DECENTRALISED MANAGEMENT OF EDUCATION

Mangement of Education in Panchayati Raj and Municipal Bodies

DECENTRALISED MANAGEMENT OF EDUCATION

Mangement of Education in Panchayati Raj and Municipal Bodies

Editor

Dr. DIGURMARTI BHASKARA RAO

M.Sc., M.A., M.A., M.Ed., Ph.D.

R.V.R. College of Education

Guntur-522006

Andhra Pradesh

India

2001

DISCOVERY PUBLISHING HOUSE

New Delhi

First Published-2001
Reprinted-2011
ISBN 81-7141-617-9

Published by :
DISCOVERY PUBLISHING HOUSE
4831/24, Ansari Road, Prahlad Street,
Darya Ganj, New Delhi-110002 (INDIA)
✆ : 3279245 • Fax : 91-11-3253475
E-mail : dphtemp@indiatimes.com

Prited at : Dynamic Printers, Delhi

CONTENTS

PREFACE

The National Policy on Education (1986) and its Programme of Action gave unqualified priority to Universalisation of Elementary Education and introduced many innovations. Keeping in view of the Programme of Action (1992), CABE Committee was set up to formulate guidelines on decentratlised management of education in the context of 73rd and 74th Constitutional Amendment Acts and it made recommendations regarding the management of education at district, sub-district and village levels in Panchayati Raj bodies and Municipal bodies.

The report of the CABE Committee on Decentralised Management; National Policy on Education Part X, The Management of Education; Programme of Action (1992), Extracts from the Chapter on Management of Education; copy of the Constitution (Seventy-third Amendment) Act, 1992; and copy of the Constitution (Seventy-fourth Amendment) Act, 1992 presented in their original form in this book will help the educational personnel in achieving the Indian dream "Universalisation of Elementary Educaiton".

Thanks are due to Department of Education, Ministry of Human Resource Development, Government of India for reproducing these documents in this book for the benefit of elite and mass.

D. Bhaskara Rao
Independence Day of India

ACKNOWLEDGEMENT

The CABE Committee on Decentralised Management of Education is deeply indebted to the Government of Karnataka for the excellent convention facilities offered by them for holding the meetings both in Delhi and in Bangalore. A special word of thanks is due to Shri K. P. Singh, Resident Commissioner, and Shri D. N. Nayak, Deputy Resident Commissioner, Government of Karnataka, New Delhi.

The Committee expresses its deep appreciation of the invaluable contribution made by Shri P. K. Umashankar, but for him finalization of this report would not have been possible in such a short time.

The Committee wishes to place on record its sincere appreciation of the contribution made by Shri Baldev Mahajan, Joint Director, NIEPA and Dr. S. C. Nuna, Fellow, NIEPA in preparing the documents for the Committee.

The Committee further expresses its grateful appreciation of the outstanding work done by the Member-Secretary Dr. R. V. Vaidyanatha Ayar, Joint Secretary, Department of Education.

Secretarial assistance and administrative support for the meetings of the Committee were provided in an impeccable manner by a dedicated team comprising S/Shri T. C. James, B. K. Ray, Krishan Kumar, Kum. Basobi Sircar, Smt. Anajana Saluja, S/Shri S. R. Gupta, S. K. Jain, Hakim Singh, Jai Prakash, Smt. Sarla Arya, S/Shri P. K. Theraja, A. K. Khurana, E. Krishna Kumaran, Padam Singh, S. K. Dagar, J. S. Aswal, Satbir Singh, V. Nagarajan, S. Raghvendran, Chiranji Lal, Gorakhnath Yadav, S. S. Butola and Shiv Dayal. The Committee is grateful to them all

ABBREVIATIONS

CABE	Central Advisory Board of Education
DIET	District Institute of Education and Training
ECCE	Early Childhood Care and Education
HRD	Human Resource Development
NCERT	National Council of Education Research and Training
NFE	Non-formal Eduction
NIEPA	National Institute of Educational Planning and Administration
NPE	National Policy on Education
PEC	Panchayat Standing Committee on Education
POA	Programme of Action
PRI	Panchayati Raj Institution
PSEC	Panchayat Samiti Standing Committee on Education
SABE	State Advisory Board of Education
SCERT	State Council of Educational Research and Training
SIE	State Institute of Education
VEC	Village Education Committee
ZPEC	Zilla Parishad Standing Committee on Education

CHAPTER I

THE BACKGROUND

Directive Principle

The Panchayati Raj system is not new to India. The Panchayats have functioned in varying forms of centuries in different parts of the country. Gandhiji wished to revive the Panchayati Raj Institutions (PRIs) in the 20th century with democratic bases of their own and by investing in them adequate powers to ensure that the villagers could have a real sense of *Swaraj.* The introduction of Article 40 in the Constitution of India which states that 'the State shall take steps to organise village panchayats and endow them with such powers and authority as may be necessary to enable them to function as units of self-government' was a step towards this direction. This Article formed a part of the Directive Principles of the State policy under the Constitution.

Community Development Programme

After independence India has strived to accelerate the process of development through active participation of the people at the grass-root level. The decentralization of socio-economic development programmes was conceptualized as early as the First Five Year Plan. It was envisaged that the villages would undertake and execute the programmes of development with actual support of the State. Accordingly, it was felt necessary to change the structure of development administration. Launching of Community Development Programme in 1952 was a first step in this direction.

Development was conceived as an integrated process. A need was felt for building development administration which is sensitive to the aspirations and needs of the people. This led to creation of development blocks.

The community development programme was thought to be a pioneering step in the process of decentralised planning. It was expected to induce transformation in the rural areas with focus on agriculture. However, it was soon realised that it had not been able to serve the purpose, to a large extent, because of excessive bureaucratic control. In many ways, it was felt that the programme had not been able to come to terms with people's aspirations. As a result it failed to mobilise and involve the rural masses in taking decisions about the activities which affect their lives directly.

Evolution of Panchayati Raj Institutions

The significance of decentralization in accelerating the process of development was emphasised by the Balwantrai Mehta Committee (1957) which was set-up to make recommendations on new structures to be created to involve local people in the development process. The committee recommended the "establishment of an interconnected three-tier organisational structure of democratic decentralization at the village, block and district levels".

The Panchayati Raj Acts were enacted in most of the states in fifties. While the pattern suggested by Balwantrai Mehta Committee was generally followed in most of the States, there were some local variations, the most significant being the primacy given to the district tier in the states of Maharashtra and Gujarat by having strong Zilla Parishads with considerable administrative powers. Notwithstanding the local variations, there was general acceptance of the need to decentralise political and administrative power. Subsequently, Panchayati Raj legislations were amended in a number of states to give greater responsibilities to Panchayati Raj bodies to accelerate the process of development.

The interest and support for Panchayati Raj, however, did not last long due to various reasons. After the mid-sixties, the process of decline was visible. The flow of funds for block development was reduced to a trickle after the close of the intensive stage of the community development programme. In many States tendency to postpone the Panchayati Raj elections indefinitely was also noticeable. Simultaneously, parallel bodies came to be set-up at the district level in some States, thus reducing the role of the Panchayati Raj Institutions in development planning and implementation.

Constitutional Provisions

The Constitution (73rd Amendment) Act, 1992 envisages States to establish a three-tier system of strong, viable and responsive Panchayats at the village, intermediate and district levels. Similarly, the Constitution (74th Amendment) Act, 1992 envisages to establish the Municipalities in the urban areas. States are expected to devolve adequate powers, responsibilities and finances upon these bodies so as to enable them to prepare plans and implement schemes for economic development and social justice. These Acts provide a basic framework of decentralisation of powers and authorities to the Panchayati Raj/Municipal bodies at different levels. However, responsibility for giving it a practical shape rests with the States. States are expected to act in consonance with the spirit of the Acts for establishing a strong and viable system of local self-government.

The 73rd and 74th Amendments to the Constitution of India constitute a new chapter in the process of democratic decentralisation in India. In terms of these Amendments, the responsibility for taking decisions regarding activities at the grass-root level which affect people's lives directly would rest upon the elected members of the people themselves. By making regular elections to Panchayati Raj/Municipal bodies mandatory, these institutions have been given their due place in the demoractic set-up of the country. Stage has come to make these bodies an organic part of the development process in the country.

Presently 16 States/UTs have got three-tier system (with some modifications in Tamil Nadu and Assam), 5 States/UTs have two-tier system and 8 States/UTs have only single tier system of Panchayats. Article 243(b)(1) of the Act envisages that all the States/UTs, except those with population not exceeding 20 lakhs, will have to constitute a three-tier system of panchayats i.e. at the village, intermediate and district levels. While the district has been defined as a normal district in a State, the jurisdiction of village and intermediate level have not been specifically defined in the Act. Village as per the provisions of the Act is to be specified by the Governor by a public notification for the purpose of this part and includes a group of villages so specified. That means the territorial area of a village panchayat can be specified by a public notification by the Governor of the State, and may consist of more than one village. Similarly, intermediate level which can be a taluk, block or a mandal, is also to be specified by the Governor through a public notification in this regard. This provides certain amount of flexibility to the States in constituting Panchayats at the lower and the middle level.

Participative Management

The basic function of democratic decentralization is to ensure that the development planning is more responsive and adaptable to regional and local needs of the population. It ensures people's participation—the fact recognised by all for the success of development programmes. Further, it is also based on the premises that the people at the grass root levels have a better perception of their requirements. However, the system of local self-government goes a step further by ensuring delegation of political power. It also ensures involving objects of development in directing and executing the development activities—an indispensable aspect to improve the effectiveness of programme. Therefore, planning and implementation of development programmes by people's participation in political and developmental processes constitutes a significant aspect of Panchayati Raj/Municipal bodies.

Education under Panchayati Raj

The Panchayati Raj/Municipal bodies have an important role to play in reconstruction of the education system. It is being realised that there is an alienation between the community in general and educational system and thus efforts towards ensuring larger enrolment, raising retention, rate and improving teaching-learning process, have not succeeded substantially.

The establishment of Institutions of local self-government may be seen as a significant step in the direction of making the system more effective as well as responsive. The Panchayati Raj/ Municipal bodies ought to make responsible for planning, execution and monitoring of various educational programmes at different levels. It may not be out of place to mention that the National Policy on Education and the Programme of Action (1992) emphasise the importance of the decentralisation of planning and management of education at all levels of ensuring greater community participation.

While transferring various functions to institutions of local self-government, the approach must be tempered with caution and mature deliberations. These institutions may not grow immediately into their full potential and start performing the extremely ambitious and complex tasks. Keeping in view the relative weaknesses of the Panchayati Raj/Municipal bodies, their limited resources and complex nature of their responsibilities, they need to be nurtured, supported and encouraged in a positive manner. The positive partnership between Panchayati Raj/Municipal bodies and State governments will go a long way in confronting the multifaceted tasks of educational development.

CHAPTER II

CABE COMMITTEE ON DECENTRALISED MANAGEMENT OF EDUCATION

Constitution and Deliberations

National Policy on Education (NPE)

The provision of free and compulsory education to all children until they complete the age of 14 years is a Directive Principle of the Constitution. Determined efforts have been made towards achieving this goal since 1950. The National Policy on Education (1986) and its Programme of Action gave unqualitifed priority to universalisation of elementary education and introduced many innovations. The micro-level planning has been conceived as a strategy to achieve this objective which focusses on "family-wise and child-wise plan of action" by which "every child regularly attend school or NFE centres, continues his/her education at the places suitable to him/her and completes atleast 8 years of schooling or its equivalent at the non-formal centre".

The National Policy on Education comprehensively charts the future course of educational development. While recognising the pivotal role of the Centre and States in the management of education, it advocates establishment of Distric Boards of Education. It envisages that :

"District Boards of Education will be created to manage education up to higher secondary level. State Governments will attend to this aspect with all possible expedition. Within the multi-level framework of educational development, Centre, State, District and local level agencies will participate in planning, coordination, monitoring and evaluation".

Programme of Action (POA)

A land-mark development that followed the formulation of the National Policy on Education (1986) was the preparation of "Programme of Action" (POA) presenting the detailed operational strategies for the implementation of the policy. The POA under the theme of Management of Education advocated the creation of District Boards of Education with the responsibility for implementation of all educational programmes including school, non-formal and adult education upto the higher secondary level. The POA postulates that "the Boards will also be vested with the responsibility for planning which would include *inter alia,* area development, spatial planning, institutional planning, administrative and financial control and personnel management with respect to primary, middle, secondary and higher secondary schools". The POA also envisaged appropriate statutory authority for the District Boards. In view of the fact that the management of education upto secondary level was proposed to be transferred to Panchayati Raj bodies, it was later felt that the concept of the District Boards of Education needs to be substituted by the decentralized administrative set-up that might be created under the Panchayati Raj bodies.

Central Advisory Board of Education (CABE)

The CABE revised the Programme of Action in 1992 taking cognisance of the developments since 1986. It took note of the Constitutional Amendment Bills introduced in the Parliament on Panchayati Raj and Municipal bodies, envisaging setting up of democratically elected bodies at district, sub-district panchayat and municipality levels. Noting that the Amendment bills were enabling legislations, the POA observed that the States would need to draw up appropriate legislation which among other things must provide for Panchayati Raj Committees on Education. The POA observed that it would be necessary for the Ministry of Human Resource Development to prepare model statutory provisions for the guidance of the States when they formulate their legislation under the Panchayati Raj Acts.

Since then, the Constitution has been amended for establishing regular democratically bodies at the village, intermediate, district and municipality levels. The Constitution provides the pattern of election to these bodies and their tenure. It also provides for the state legislature to legislate suitably in other areas including entrustment of functions to the Panchayati Raj/Municipal bodies, which among other things include, in the case of rural areas, " Education including primary and secondary schools, technical training and vocational education adult and non-formal education" and in the case of municipalities "promotion of cultural, educational and aesthetic aspects".

CABE Committee

Keeping in view the recommendations of the POA, the Minister of Human Resource Development, in his capacity as the Chairman of the CABE, set up a CABE Committee, under the Chairmanship of Shri M. Veerappa Moily, the Chief Minister of Karnataka, to formulate guidelines on decentralised management of education in the context of 73rd and 74th Constitutional Amendment Acts. The Committee under its terms of reference was to formulate guidelines for the management of education at district, sub-district and village levels keeping in view the 73rd and 74th Amendments to the Constitution of India.

The Department of Education, Ministry of Human Resource Development set up a Core Group at NIEPA, comprising Shri P.K. Uma Shankar, Shri Baldev Mahajan and Dr. S.C. Nuna, for assisting the CABE Committee in its deliberations. The Core Group assisted the Committee in its deliberations by preparing a number of documents, background papers and materials for the use of the Committee.

First Meeting of the Committee

The Committee held its first meeting on 26th April, 1993, in New Delhi. It deliberated on the methods and procedures to be adopted for its functioning. The Committee had following documents before it.

1. *National Policy on Education* (Revised, 1992)
2. Extracts from the *Programme of Action* (1992) to implement the National Policy on Education
3. Seventy-third and Seventy-fourth Constitutional Amendment Acts
4. Documents published by the National Institute of Rural Development, Hyderabad on Panchayati Raj:
   a. *Summary of major Reports on Panchayati Raj*
   b. *Salient Features of Panchayati Raj Acts*
   c. *Structural Patterns*
5. Documents prepared by the Core Group:
   a. "Panchayati Raj bodies and Development: A Perspective"
   b. "Experience of Panchayati Raj bodies in the field of Education in the States of Andhra Pradesh, Gujarat, Karnataka, Maharastra and Uttar Pradesh".
   c. "Issues to be considered by the CABE Committee while formulating its Recommendation on the Decentralized Management of Education under the Panchayati Raj bodies".

The Chief Minister of Karnataka, presiding over the first meeting, welcomed the participants and highlighted the importance of decentralisation of the educational management. He emphasised that the decentralisation is the key to achieve optimum results in the system of education and explained the importance of restructuring the entire management system of education in the backdrop of structural readjustment of the economy. Shri Moily laid special stress on participative democracy and said decentralisation was the effective way to ensure education aimed at growth with social justice.

The Committee during its deliberations, noted that decentralisation did not mean mere delegation of powers; it meant entrustment of certain responsibilities. The educational management has to be a movement of the people. The Panchayati Raj bodies may ensure convergence of services and prevention of fragmentation of work and responsibilities. The Committee also observed that modern administrative methods and practices should included in the Panchayati Raj system. The Committee also noted that the decentralised management structures should facilitate in achieving the naticnal goals of universalisation of elementary education and total adult literacy.

There was also a note of caution. It was felt that hasty decentralisation of management of education should be avoided. Need for detailed and indepth studies regarding areas and subjects to be transferred to the Panchayati Raj bodies was also emphasized. The States would have to work out the details, though the Programme of Action provides the guidelines. Some subjects would lend themselves for decentralisation while others like formulation of syllabus, preparation of text books etc. may have to be the responsibility of the States. It was also observed that the Panchayati Raj bodies may require time to equip themselves for the work and decentralisation may proceed slowly and cautiously but surely. The objective of decentralisation must be to administer with greater efficiency.

At the conclusion of the first meeting, the Committee decided that the views and opinions of the States and Union Territories on decentralised management of education should be obtained and should be available at the next meeting of the Committee. The Committee desired that background notes should be elaborated giving more details about the experience of the States as well as of other countries in the field of decentralised management. The Committee indicated that it would finalise the issues to be considered by the Committee at the next meeting after perusal of all the documents.

Second Meeting of the Committee

The Committee held its second meeting on 10th June, 1993 at Bangalore. The Committee had before it the following documents:

1. Detailed reports on Structure, Role and Functions of Panchayati Raj Institutions in the States of Andhra Pradesh, Gujarat, Karnataka and Maharasthra.

2. Papers on different aspects of decentralisation in England, France, Scandinavian countries, Papua New Guinea and Nigeria.
3. A Note containing revised issues to be considered by the Committee.
4. Comments of the States and Union Territories in response to the communication from the Chairman seeking their views.

During the discussions, it was observed that the decentralised management of education will have far reaching bearing on educational development in the country and hence calls for deliberations in depth. Decentralisation of management was needed not only to improve the quality of education, but also in view of the fact that educational system has become too large and the aspirations of the people can be met only under a decentralised system. It was also noted that the institutional strategies like the Village Education Committee to secure involvement of people should be given importance. While the new system must be cost effective, at the same time, educational administration at district and sub-district level would need to be strengthened. Nomination of professionals would be a step towards providing professional orientation to the Panchayati Raj bodies and building up their credibility. Decentralisation as the means for greater participation of people in the process of educational development is a welcome move. These bodies have manifold responsibilities and they would require financial and administrative support for managing education. Mistakes in education would have long term consequences. Experiments in the past failed because of the lack of planning and financial constraints. The Panchayati Raj bodies would need to be adequately supported and strengthened before giving them additional responsibilities.

The Committee identified the following issues for detailed discussion at the next meeting:

(i) The education subjects that could be delegated to the Panchayati Raj bodies in the context of 11th Schedule of the 73rd Constitutional Amendment and the *inter se* distribution of the delegated subjects among the 3-tiers of Panchayati Raj, having regard to:

(a) The need to balance the requirements of uniformity and standardisation on one hand and of participatory management and decentralisaiton on the other.

(b) The imperative of providing basic education services of satisfactory quality.

(ii) The structures to be created at the Panchayat, Panchayat Samiti and Zilla Parishad levels for the management of education; their composition, powers and functions.

(iii) The powers to be delegated to the Panchayati Raj bodies in regard to educational institutions not managed by the local bodies or the state governments.

(iv) The procedure of recruitment of teaching and non-teaching staff and the extent to which such recruitment, transfer and service conditions could be delegated to the Panchayati Raj bodies.

(v) The powers and functions in regard to administrative and academic supervision of educational institutions that could be delegated to the Panchayati Raj bodies.

(vi) The extent of flexibility which may be provided to the Panchayati Raj bodies in regard to various norms and standards that would be laid down at the state level such as sanctioning of schools, teacher-pupil ratio, appointment of teachers, fees, incentive, curricula, syllabi, text-books, supplementary reading, examination, academic calendar, and curricular, co-curricular and extra curricular activities etc.

(vii) The measures for coordination and integration between the activities undertaken at different levels so that holistic perception informs educational management.

(viii) Mechanisms for providing adequate financial resources tot he Panchayati Raj bodies to discharge activities vested in them.

(ix) Financial consequences of delegation of powers to Panchayati Raj bodies.

(x) Strategy for progressively entrusting Panchayati Raj bodies with more functions and powers in the field of education.

(xi) Training of Panchayati Raj functionaries, political and administrative, in the planning and management of education.

(xii) The components of a model legislation in regard to the management of education by Panchayati Raj bodies.

(xiii) Similar issues in regard to management of education in urban areas.

Third Meeting of the Committee

The third meeting of the Committee was held on 17th July, 1993 in New Delhi. The Chairman emphasised the need for finalising the Report at the earliest as the States are in the process of preparing necessary legislation under the constitutional provisions of the Panchayati Raj Act. The Committee also noted that decentralisation has been in the force in one form or the other in the country since 1956 and decentralised structures in education had existed even earlier in the form of District Boards. It was also observed that the decentralisation cannot be uniform throughout the country. However, measures to ensure people's participation can be common to all the States. It was also felt that the Panchayati Raj bodies would be necessary to achieve the convergence of related areas like early childhood care and education, primary education and vocational education at the ground level. The necessity to generate resources for education of people was also reiterated. It was felt that the people may willingly contribute if they were given the power.

Dr. P. V. Ranga Rao, Minister of Education, Andhra Pradesh made a brief presentation to the Committee on the "Views of the State Level Seminar on Management of Education." The main recommendations of the Seminar were:

1. Constitution of VEC as a statutory body at the Village level with functions and responsibilities as enlisted in the *Report of the Seminar.*

2. Constitution of District Board of Education as an autonomous, statutory body at the District level with a broad based composition to look-after Upper Primary and Secondary Stages of education with District Education Officer as Member-Convenor and Chief Executive Officer.

3. Academic and Technical supervision to be exclusive function of Education Department with Education Officers at the district and lower level.

4. State Education Department to be responsible for all matters concerned with pre-service, and in-service training of teachers; maintaining uniformity of standards in education; prescription of curriculum; printing and distribution of textbooks; conduct of examinations and issue of certificates etc.

The Committee also considered the suggestions received from the various State Governments/Union Territories Administration, and other Institutions in response to the Chairman's communication.

The Committee noted that the varied experience of the States should be taken into account for preparing future action plans. It was also felt that the recommendations of the Committee should be wise as well as practical. Although there was an unanimity on the need to increase the budgetary allocation but how to raise the resources was a critical issue. The lack of administrative support for the PRIs was also referred to. While it may be possible to involve the Panchayats in the literacy and, non-formal education programmes, total responsibility for formal education may be a difficult task. The recommendations of the Committee, it was felt, may have to be broad-based and flexible; indicative rather than prescriptive. The States should have freedom to choose the model which suits their situation.

The Committee felt that while setting up a Village Education Committee, its conflict with the Panchayats should be avoided. The people who are knowledgeable about education should be involved in these bodies. Members of the bodies at the lower levels should find representation in the bodies at the higher level. The experience of some of the States suggest that people at different levels need to be prepared to assume the responsibilities and exercise of the powers which may be delegated to them. The Committee also felt that it should be ensured that the quality of education does not go down because of the decentralisation. All the proposals should be viable. While resources would need to be raised, optimum utilisation of resources will have to be ensured. Organisational support need to be built into the structures along with accountability and cooperation.

The Committee observed that in order to secure effective participation of the people, there was a need for broad-based participative structures for education as distinct from the general Panchayati Raj structures. While there would be commonality of some membership between the Panchayati Raj structures and those dealing with education, the latter will have to have members from the educational field and other interest groups like parent-teachers associations and members of the disadvantaged sections, etc.

Basically institutions serving primary education, non-formal education, adult education and ECCE should come within the scope of the Village Education Committee. Education at the upper primary level should be the area of responsibility of the Panchayat Samiti Standing Committee on Education and Secondary Education that of the Zilla Parishad Standing Committee on Education. The Committee generally agreed with the proposals made in the statements circulated in the meeting with certain modifications generally agreed with the proposals made in the statements circulated in the meeting with certain modifications.

Fourth Meeting of the Committee

The fourth meeting of the CABE Committee was held on 9th August, 1993, in New Delhi to consider the draft report of the Committee which was circulated to the members in advance. The draft report provided for setting up the Village Education Committee in each village with statutory authority. The opinion of the Ministry of Law was sought on this issue. The Ministry was of the view that within the jurisdiction of a Panchayat only one Committee dealing with education may be set up. It was clarified that the

Panchayat may, however, set up a Village Eduction Committee in each village as a sub-committee of the Panchayat. The Committee agreed on this proposal for constituting Village Education Committee as a sub-committee of the Panchayat where Panchayat comprises a group of villages. However, in the situation where Panchayat comprises only a single village, a Panchayat Standing Committee on education may be set up.

Keeping in view the village situation, the Committee felt that instead of having an "educationist from the village" on the Committee "a person having interest in education" may by nominated. The committee also agreed that atleast one-third of the members of the Standing Committee at various levels should be women. The VEC may also be given power to nominate non-elected members of the different categories on the Committee. The Committee felt that the states should delegate the powers regarding the implementation of various programmes through appropriate sub-ordinate legislation. It was felt that at intermediate level, the process of supervision should be brought closer to the schools and for that purpose supervisory staff of the education department at the block/taluk level should be placed with the Panchayati Raj bodies.

A view was offered that the transfer of teaching and non-teaching staff to Panchayati Raj bodies may create problems as employees generally want to remain in Government service. The Committee however, felt that the teaching and supervisory staff in Government service could be deputed to Panchayati Raj bodies. In case of appointments, a panel could be provided to the Zilla Parishad. The salary of the staff could be paid from Zilla Parishad funds, received from Government and other agencies.

The Committee suggested that the members of the Standing Committees at the lower level of Panchayati Raj bodies should be represented in the Committee at the higher levels.

With respect to management of Education in the Municipal areas, it was felt that the primary schools may be placed under the control of the Municipal bodies, while secondary and higher secondary schools could remain with the Government or be placed under the control of a Municipal body depending on the specific situations.

Fifth Meeting of the Committee

The fifth meeting of the Committee was held on 20th August, 1993, to finalise its report. The Committee felt that the issues related to personnel management are of complex nature and therefore, a cautious approach should be followed. It was felt that transfer of teaching and non-teaching employees to Panchayati Raj bodies in the present circumstances may not be viable in some states. However, their services could be placed with the Panchayati Raj bodies. It was also suggested that the timely disbursement of salary to all the employees should be ensured.

Shri S. S. Chakraborty, Education Minister, West Bengal while appreciating the spirit underlying the decentralisation of educational management, reiterated certain points. He drew attention of the Committee to the fact that in West Bengal education is run by democratically elected and representative bodies like State Board of Primary Education, District Primary Education Council, West Bengal Board of Secondary Education, etc. The State Government was also considering evolving of a procedure so that the Panchayat can play its due role in the management of formal and informal education. While agreeing with the formation of the Village Education Committee, Shri Chakraborty pointed out that it cannot be a separate committee. He also said that instead of transferring employees from the Directorate of Education to Panchayats, their services may be placed with the Panchayati Raj bodies wherever necessary. He reiterated that panchayat should not be the recruiting authority of teachers but it should have the supervisory right; recruitment, transfer and disciplinary authority should rest with the academic bodies which will give due consideration to the recommendations of the panchayats. He also said that the prescription of curricula, preparation of textbooks, conduct of examinations and issue of certificates should be with the academic body. He strongly emphasised the need for appropriate financial allocation to the decentralised structures.

The Committee stressed the need for having effective control over the teaching and non-teaching staff to ensure better quality of education the ultimate objective of decentralised educational management is to improve the standard of teaching and learning.

While considering the issues of personnel management, the Committee felt that the State Governments may suitably adapt the recommendations of the Committee, keeping in view the spirit of the Constitutional Amendments to suit the local conditions. It was also suggested that the Central Government should consider setting up of an appropriate financial institution for the development and maintenance of infrastructure in the schools under the Panchayati Raj bodies.

The Committee approved the report with modifications suggested by the Committee.

CHAPTER III

Guiding Principles

Role of Panchayati Raj

Education in the country is at a crucial stage of development. Despite phenomenal progress since independence, the objectives of universalisation of elementary education and total literacy still remain elusive goals. The problem of irregular attendance of children and their subsequent drop-out in large numbers continues to be a cause for concern. Another matter for concern is the slow progress in providing education to the disadvantaged sections of population, such as, girls, children belonging to Scheduled Castes, Scheduled Tribes, backward classes and minorities. All these issues pose a serious challenge for the management of education. The Committee recognises that decentralisation of educational management under the institutions of local self-government would ensure active and greater participation of people and their representatives. However, keeping in view the challenging nature of the tasks ahead, the Panchayati Raj/Municipal bodies would require adequate preparation and strengthening before they are called upon to perform the new roles and functions.

Administrative Support

The Panchayati Raj/Municipal bodies in some of the states are still relatively inexperienced in the tasks of administration. Their members are mostly part-time voluntary workers who are being called upon to shoulder a wide range of complex responsibilities. There is obvious need for capability building of elected members of the Panchayati Raj bodies for performing their functions through periodic orientation programmes, and through interaction with political leadership and departmental officers at different levels. With the responsibility for management of educational institutions and programmes, they must be given the necessary administrative and professional support through appropriate departmental structures. The existing departmental and administrative structures of the State at these levels will have to be placed at the disposal of the Panchayati Raj/Municipal bodies. They would also have to be strengthened whereever necessary.

The administration of educational programmes would require professional support. Hence, the Panchayati Raj/Municipal bodies which are entrusted with specific educational responsibilities should have representation of experts and educationists for providing a professional orientation to their tasks.

Finances

The finances of the institutions of local self-government constitute the weakest link. While they may become cost-effective with growing experience and confidence, in the initial stage they would require financial and resource support from the State Government and the Centre. The allocations that the centre and State provide for the different programmes and activities which may be transferred to the Panchayati Raj/Municipal bodies, should be made available in full to these bodies. There would also be a need for additional financial support to make these Institutions viable. At the same time, it is also necessary that the pattern of such financial assistance must result in cost-effectiveness and efficiency, right from the initial phase. Generation of their own resources should be suitably rewarded with matching grants.

Teaching Community

Education is a sensitive area. The academic community is the most important constituent of the educational programmes. The Panchayati Raj/Municipal bodies must be sensitised to the need for handling educational cadres with restraint, imagination, sympathy and genuine understanding. The past experience indicates that the teaching community has not always been happy in its interactions with the Panchayati Raj bodies. Issues relating to recruitment and transfers seem to have created misunderstanding between these bodies and teaching community. While the role of Panchayati Raj bodies in ensuring effective and regular functioning of schools is significant, they have to recognise and appreciate the role of teachers. The State would need to lay down clear guidelines with respect to various aspects of personnel management, particularly norms for posting and transfers of teachers.

Professional Support

While the Panchayati Raj bodies should be able to secure community participation, educational progress would require professional inputs and support. The Panchayati Raj bodies must be enabled to build their links with professional institutions and voluntary organisations and seek their support and assistance in promoting their educational efforts. Evaluation of progress, formulation of perspective plans, preparation of innovative schemes, organisation of surveys and such other educational tasks will require professional inputs. The State Departments of Education must assist the Panchayati Raj/Municipal bodies to develop appropriate mechanism for securing professional inputs and support.

Delegation of Functions

While the Constitution provides for the establishment of Panchayati Raj/Municipal bodies and holding of regular elections as mandate, it allows discretion to the State legislatures in deciding about the functions and powers to be delegated to these bodies. The composition of these bodies have been left to the discretion of the State Government. While formulating guidelines for the States regarding the composition of various bodies under these institutions, the Committee's proposals are mainly derived from the Constitutional provisions, the National Policy on Education and the Programme of Action. These guidelines are in the nature of a broad framework which has to be elaborated and developed by the States in the light of their varying situations. The proposals of the Committee are intended to facilitate the work of the State Governments in deciding the issues in their own context. Ultimately, the States are free to choose their own structures, determine their own schedules of functions and powers to be delegated to the Panchayati Raj/Municipal bodies keeping in view the spirit underlying the Constitutional Amendments. The Committee is well aware that there can be no single model for all the States. The extent of powers to be entrusted to the Panchayati Raj/Municipal bodies may vary from state to state depending upon their past experience, present perceptions and circumstances and future requirements. The Committee has attempted to make the proposals as comprehensive and detailed as possible so that the States may have an opportunity to assess all the details for their own course of action, best suited to their needs and circumstances.

Role of State Governments and other Agencies

The State Governments, the Departments of Education, professional institutions, voluntary organisations and Panchayati Raj/Municipal bodies must become partners in the task of educational reconstruction. The State Governments must provide requisite support, guidance and advice; the education departments must extend professional support and administrative assistance; the professional organisations and voluntary efforts may provide the necessary insights; while the Panchayati Raj/Municipal bodies would secure the community backing and mobilisation. Rival roles and negative responses have no place in these efforts. The ultimate success of Panchayati Raj/Municipal bodies in development of education will depend upon how well the Centre, the States and the Departments provide support and guidance to these bodies for their development along the best lines.

Perspective

Local self-government is not a new development in our country. Villages in ancient India were very effective instruments of self governance. Even during the British rule, District Boards played a significant role in educational development. Subsequently, the Panchayati Raj movement was launched to accelerate the process of development. While the record of educational management under the Panchayati Raj bodies has been mixed, perhaps for reasons which are largely political, some of the states have shown good results. Recently, some states which have established Panchayati Raj bodies, have reported an encouraging progress. It is increasingly becoming evident that bureaucratic systems are not able to manage the challenges in the field of educational development and the people's participation is seen the world over an essential pre-requisite for achieving the goal of education for all. It is in this context that the Committee perceives the entrustment of educational programmes to institutions of local self-government as a step in the right direction.

CHAPTER IV

RECOMMENDATIONS

Constitutional Provisions

The Committee in its deliberations has been guided by the provisions of the Seventy-third, and the Seventy-fourth Constitutional Amendment Acts, the National Policy on Education and Programme of Action (1992). The recommendations of the Committee are in the nature of guidelines, which may be considered as comprehensive though not exhaustive. The States may after due consultations and deliberations choose a pattern and system suited to their needs and keeping in view the spirit of the Constitutional amendments and need to foster people's participation if educational goals are to be achieved. While the states which are delegating powers to the institutions of local self-government for the first time may prefer to proceed cautiously, those States which have already gained experiences in this sphere may decide to improve on these proposals and give higher levels of responsibilities to Panchayati Raj/Municipal bodies.

The Constitution makes a mandatory provision for establishment of Panchayats at the village, intermediate and district levels in each state. Keeping in view the three-tier structure (States with population below 20 lakhs need not have the intermediate tier) these proposals envisage delegation of responsibilities of educational management to the Panchayats, Panchayat Samitis and Zilla Parishads. A summary of the Committee's recommendations in this regard is presented in respect of (a) Panchayats where jurisdiction is limited to one village, (b) Panchayats where jurisdiction extends to a group of villages, (c) Panchayat Samitis (intermediate level) and (d) Zilla Parishads (district level), in Statements (IA, IB, II and III, respectively. Detailed description of the recommendations is contained in the subsequent paragraphs of this chapter.

Panchayat Level

For the purpose of defining the jurisdiction of the Panchayat, the village is to be specified by the Governor by a public notification, and may include a group of villages so specified. A Panchayat area means a territorial area of a Panchayat. This implies that Panchayat at the Village level may comprise a village or a group of villages.

The Programme of Action approved by the CABE attaches considerable importance to Village Education Committees (VECs). The village normally represents a cohesive community and is ideally suited for promoting programme, involving support of the community, such as, Early Childhood Care and Education, Primary Eduction, Non-formal Education and Adult Education. VEC may be considered the ideal organisation to mobilise and involve people in the educational efforts.

Panchayat Standing Committee on Education

The Education Committee at the Panchayat level where the panchayat comprises only one village can be named as the Panchayat Standing Committee on Education (PEC). It can be given statutory authority by bringing it under the Panchayati Raj legislation. The tenure of this Committee will be the same as the tenure of the Panchayat.

Composition

The Panchayat Standing Committee on Education may consist of not less than 7 and not more than 15 members. It may be headed by the Chairman of the Panchayat. At least one third of its members should be women. One member each representing Scheduled Castes, Scheduled Tribes, backward classes and minorities should also be on the Committee. A parent representative

PROPOSED PANCHAYATI RAJ STRUCTURES FOR MANAGEMENT OF EDUCATION AND THEIR RESPONSIBILITIES

STATEMENT - IA : PANCHAYAT LEVEL WHERE PANCHAYAT COMPRISES SINGLE VILLAGE

Proposed Structure for Management of Education and its Composition	*Role and Functions*	*Powers*	*Funds*	*Organisational and Administrative Support*	*Preparation and Training Requirements*
Panchayat Standing Committee on Education (PEC) comprising not less than 7 and not more than 15 members, including Chairman of Panchayat One member of SC, ST, BC and Minorities A representative of PTA (Parent) An Anganwai worker A person interested in education	Supervision over adult education, early childhood care and education, non-formal and primary education. Supervision over composite upper-primary schools under delegation of authority from Panchayat Samiti Generation and Sustenance of awareness among the village community ensuring participation of all segments of population Promote enrolment drives in primary schools and persuade parents of non-attending children to send their wards to schools Reduce drop outs in primary schools by initiating measures and services for retention Assist in smooth functioning of primary schools Seek support of teachers, youths and	To visit educational institutions To check attendance and other registers to enquire and report to concerned authorities on educational deficiencies and requirements in the village To recommend annual budget of school to concerned authority	Funds provided by State govts., Zilla Parishad and Panchayat Samiti Earmarked funds provided by concerned agencies of State government Funds locally raised from parents and public	Assistance of Headmaster and teachers in Government schools	Orientation/ training of PEC members, teachers and Headmasters

Contd...

1	2	3	4	5	6
Member Secretary—Head-master of Primary/Upper Primary schools.	women and others for educational and other linked health and welfare programmes	To undertake construction and repair works entrusted to them			
Note;	Mobilize resources and help schools to have water supply, urinals, play grounds and other facilities				
1. Members, other than elected Panchayat members will be nominated by the Panchayat	Prepare plans and proposals within their resources for development of education in the village and to attain total adult literacy and universal primary education	To report on regularity of students, teachers attendance and school functioning			
	Present reports and proposals to Panchayat Samities and make periodic self-assessment of progress of Committee's efforts				
2. Of the total membership of the Committee, atleast one-third should be women	Coordination with other social service departments and committees for mutual support	To frame the school calendar under the guidance of the Zilla Parishad			

STATEMENT - IB : VILLAGE LEVEL WHERE PANCHAYAT COMPRISES A GROUP OF VILLAGES

Proposed Structure for Management of Education and its Composition	Role and Functions	Powers	Funds	Organisational and Administrative Support	Preparation and Training Requirements
Village Education Committee constituted by Panchayat as its Sub-Committee constituted with not less than 7 and not more than 15 members	Supervision over adult education, early childhood care and education, non-formal and primary education.	To visit educational institutions	Funds provided by State govts. Zilla Parishad and Panchayat Samiti	Assistance of Headmaster and teachers in Government schools	Orientation/ training of VEC members, teachers and Headmasters
Chairman of Panchayat or a member of Panchayat from the village concerned.	Supervision over composite upper-primary schools under delegation of authority from Panchayat Samiti	To check attendance and other registers to enquire and report to concerned authories on educational deficiencies and requirements in the village	Earmarked funds provided by concerned agencies of State government		
One member of SC, ST, BC and Minorities	Generation and Sustenance of awareness among the village community ensuring participation of all segments of population	To recommend annual budget of school to concerned authority	Funds locally raised from parents and public		
A representative of PTA (Parent)	Promote enrolment drives in primary schools and persuade parents of non-attending children to send their wards to schools	To undertake construction			
An Anganwadi worker	Reduce drop outs in primary schools by initiating measures and services for retention				
A person	Assist in smooth functioning of primary schools				
	Seek support of teachers, youths and women and others for educational and other linked health and welfare programmes				

Contd...

1	2	3	4	5	6
interested in education from the village Member Secretary—Headmaster of Primary/Upper Primary school Note: 1. Members other than elected Panchayat members will be nominated by the Panchayat from the Gram Sabha institutions in the village 2. Of the total membership of the Committee, atleast one-third should be women.	Mobilize resources and help schools to have water supply, urinals, play grounds and other facilities Prepare plans and proposals within their resources for development of education in the village and to attain total adult literacy and universal primary education Present reports and proposals to Panchayat Samities and make periodic self-assessment of progress of Committee's efforts Coordination with other social service departments and committees for mutual support	and repair works entrusted to them To report on regularity of students, teachers attendance and school functioning To frame the school calendar under the guidance of the Zilla Parishad			

STATEMENT - II : PANCHAYAT SAMITI AT INTERMEDIATE LEVEL

Proposed Structure for Management of Education and its Composition	*Role and Functions*	*Powers*	*Funds*	*Organisational and Administrative Support*	*Preparation and Training Requirements*
Panchayat Samiti Standing Committee on Education (PSEC) comprising not less than 11 and not more than 17 members. This will include. Chairman of Panchayat Samiti One member each of SC, ST, BC and Minorities One representative of PTA/NGO One or two representatives of VEC/PEC by rotation	Management of Adult Education, Non-formal Education, Early Childhood Care and Education and Govt. Primary and Upper Primary Schools under the supervision of Zilla Parishad Supervision and channelisation of grant to aided primary and upper primary schools in their jurisdiction under the guidance of Zilla Parishad. Academic supervision of all primary and upper primary schools including private schools Preparation of plans for development of education upto upper primary level in their jurisdiction Development and coordination of school complexes Coordination with other social service departments and committees for mutual support	To recruit staff for Adult Education, Non-formal Education and Early Childhood care and Education Programmes To appoint staff in schools from approved panels To transfer teachers within their jurisdiction subject to guidelines To perform academic supervision of all institutions	Grants from Zilla Parishad Grants from state/ centrally sponsored schemes through the state Earmarked funds by concerned agencies Voluntary donations, endowment trusts Funds raised through taxation by Panchayat Samiti	Services of the staff of education department at the level corresponding to the Panchayat Samiti will be placed with the Panchayat Samiti	Orientation/ training of non-official members of PSEC and officials working with them

Contd...

1	2	3	4	5	6
A Principal of Degree/Pre-degree College A Headmaster of school complex/ secondary school A representative of teachers Member Secretary-Block Education Officer or its equivalent Notes: 1. Members other than elected members of the Committee will be nominated by the Panchayat Samiti 2. Of the total membership of the		upto upper-primary level To delegate the power of supervision over composite upper-primary schools to the PEC/VEC for purpose of continuity To prepare budget and to sanction plans and expenditure plans and expenditure from the Panchayat Samiti Education Budget To channelise			

Contd...

1	2	3	4	5	6
Committee, atleast one-third should be women		funds to aided institutions under supervision of Zilla Parishad To levy development fees and other fees to raise resources. To raise public contributions and donations To propose measures to Panchayat Samiti to raise resources			

STATEMENT - III : ZILLA PARISHAD AT DISTRICT LEVEL

Proposed Structure for Management of Education and its Composition	Role and Functions	Powers	Funds	Organisational and Administrative Support	Preparation and Training Requirements
Zilla Parishad Standing Committee on Education (ZPEC) comprising not less than 15 and not more than 21 members which will include. Chairman, Zilla Parishad. A representative each of SC, ST, BC and Minorities A representative of PTA/NGO Two or more representatives of Panchayat Samiti and Panchayat Samiti and Panchayat/Village Education	Over all supervision of all educational programmes in the district upto secondary level Preparation, implementation and review of plans for development of education upto secondary level in the district Formulation and operationalisation of programmes to achieve total literacy and universal elementary education Establish and manage schools upto secondary level Academic supervision of all institutions (Govt. aided, private) upto secondary level in the district including schools in Municipalities Preparation and coordination of plans for development of education upto secondary level including those of Municipalities To review progress and guide Panchayat Samiti and Panchayat	To establish and maintain schools upto secondary level including recruitment, appointment, and transfer of staff, payment of salaries and exercise control over the staff subject to govt. guidelines To exercise control and academic supervision of all schools including aided and private schools upto secondary level	State Government grants, centrally sponsored schemes channelised through the state Earmarked funds by agencies Resources for education raised through taxation by Zilla Parishad Donations, voluntary contributions	Services of the staff of the education department at district level to be placed with the Zilla Parishad Service of the teachers working in Govt. schools will be placed with the Zilla Parishad. Their service conditions will be protected. The educational officers will continue to be under the	Orientation/ training of non-official members of ZPEC and educational functionaries Programme orientation for members of ZPEC

Contd...

1	2	3	4	5	6
Committees. Principal of a College Professor of Education from University/College Principal of D!ET A Head of school complex/ secondary school A representative of teachers Member Secretary-Chief Education Officer or equivalent Note : 1. Members other than elected members of the Committee will be nominated by the Zilla Parishad	Education Committees in their tasks Implementation of programmes for improvement of quality of education Coordination with other social service departments and committees for mutual support	subject to govt. guidelines To lay down academic and administrative norms for better functioning of educational institutions To disburse grants to aided schools subject to govt. guidelines To supervise the work of Panchayat Samiti Education Committees and Panchayat Education Committees		department and will be deputed to work with the Zilla Parishad and Panchayat Samiti. Services of the subordinate staff will also be placed with the Zilla Parishad	

Contd...

1	*2*	*3*	*4*	*5*	*6*
2. Of the total membership of the Committee, atleast one-third should be women.		To prepare and sanction educational budget To administer district educational fund To prepare perspective plan for the district To propose measures including levy of cess, surcharge and taxes for mobilising additional resources for education to the Zilla Parishad			

of the Parent-Teacher Association, the Anganwadi worker and an educationist or a person interested in education from the village may also be members of the Committee. Those members of the committee who are not elected members of the Panchayat may be nominated by the Panchyat. The Member-Secretary of the Committee will be the Headmaster of a Panchayati Raj Primary or Upper Primary School in the village and will be nominated by the Panchayat.

Role

The role of the Panchayat Standing Committee on Education may include generation and sustenance of awareness among village community ensuring participation of all segments of population, developing teacher and community partnership to oversee and manage the effective and regular functioning of the schools and centres. It should be endeavour of this Committee that every child in every family participates in primary education.

The Committee will exercise supervision over early childhood care and education, non-formal education, primary education and adult education programmes in its jurisdiction. It will also exercise supervision over composite upper primary schools under delegation of powers from the Panchayat Samiti.

Functions

The Panchayat Standing Committee on Education will be required to visit institutions and centres periodically and promote enrolment drives. Pursuading parents of non-attending children to send their wards to schools and enthusing adults for literacy programmes may form a significant agenda for its activities.

Steps to promote attendance and prevent drop-outs in the various educational programmes may also be one of the responsibilities of this Committee. It may also undertake supportive measures and services for retention of students ad will assist in the smooth functioning of the primary schools, composite upper primary schools and other institutions. It should be the Committee's endeavour to encourage and support the teachers in their tasks. It may provide essential facilities like drinking water, urinals, play-grounds, etc. in the schools. The Committee will present periodical reports and proposals to Panchayat Samiti on development of education will assess progress of the programmes in their territorial jurisdiction. It may meet as many times as required but not less than once in a quarter.

Powers

The Panchayat Standing Committee on Education will have the authority to visit educational institutions and centres providing early childhood care and education, non-formal education, primary education and adult education and will check attendance and other registers. It would also have the authority to enquire and report to the concerned authorities on educational deficiencies and requirements of the village. The Committee would recommend the annual budget of the Panchayati Raj Schools of the concerned authorities. It may report on irregularities of the attendance of students and teachers and functioning of the schools. It will prepare the school calendar indicating working days, holidays and vacation under the guidance of the Zilla Parishad.

Funds

The Committee will depend largely upon funds provided by the Zilla Parishad and Panchayat Samiti for various programmes to be undertaken in the village. It may also receive earmarked funds for specific programmes provided by concerned agencies of the State Government. The Committee may also raise funds locally from the parents and public.

Coordination

It will be desirable for VECs to hold joint meetings with similar bodies in the field of health and other subjects to seek their support in pursuance of its activities.

Administrative Support

The Village Education Committee will function largely on the basis of the staff support provided by the Headmaster, staff and teachers in the Panchayati Raj schools and other educational programmes.

Training

The members of Village Education Committees would require orientation and training for discharging their functions effectively. The Headmaster may have to be given a special orientation to enable them to assist the Village Education Committees in their activities.

Village Education Committee as Sub-Committee of Panchayat

Where the Panchayat comprises more than one village, it may establish Village Education Committee (VEC) as the sub-Committee of the Panchayat for each village. It will have statutory authority as they will be established by the Panchayats under the powers conferred upon them by the State Panchayati Raj legislation. The Panchayat may be empowered statutorily to delegate powers to these committees.

Composition

The Village Education Committee may be presided over by the President of the Panchayat where he is elected from the village. In other villages a member of the Panchayat representing the village concerned may preside over the VEC. The number of members of the VEC may be the same as provided for the Panchayat Standing Committee on Education. The composition of the Committee may also be the same, except that all the members must be drawn from the village.

The rest of the features of the Panchayat Standing Committee will also apply to the VECs (Sub-committees).

Panchayat Samiti

The Panchayat Samiti will be the Panchayati Raj body at the intermediate level in terms of the Constitutional amendment.

Panchayat Samiti Standing Committee on Education

The Panchayat Samiti may set up a Panchayat Samiti Standing Committee on Education (PSEC) for management of educational programmes in their territorial jurisdiction. This

Committee will have the statutory recognition under the Panchayati Raj legislation and will have the same tenure as the Panchayat Samiti.

Composition

The Panchayat Samiti Standing Committee on Education may be headed by the Chairman of the Panchayat Samiti. The Committee may consist of not less than 11 and not more than 17 members with atleast one-third of the members being women. One member each representing the Scheduled Castes, Scheduled Tribes, backward classes and minority communities should be on the Committee.

A parent form the Parent-Teacher Association may also be on the Committee. Atleast two representatives of the Panchayat Standing Committees on Education/Village Education Committees may be nominated by rotation. A Principal of a degree/pre-degree collage, Headmaster of a school complex/secondary school and a representative of teachers may also be on the Committee. The Member-Secretary of the Committee will be the block level Education Officer. The non-elected members of the Committee may be nominated by the Panchayat Samiti.

Role

The Panchayat Samiti Standing Committee on Education will be responsible for management of adult education non-formal education, early childhood care and education and schools of the Panchayati Raj bodies upto upper primary level, under the overall supervision of the Zilla Parishad.

All existing government schools upto upper primary level with their staff will come under the control of Panchayat Samitis and schools in the state sector will in future be established only by the Panchayat Samitis. The Committee will also have supervisory power over aided upper primary schools and will channel grant to them under the guidance of Zilla Parishad. In this regard, the committee will function in the same manner as the present departmental set-up at this level.

The Panchayat Samiti Standing Committee on Education wil undertake academic supervision of all the educational institutions upto upper primary level including the private schools in its jurisdiction.

The Education Committee at this level will endeavour to promote school complexes in its jurisdiction. The Committee will periodically review progress of education in its area and actively pursue the programmes of total adult literacy and universalisation of elementary education.

Functions

The Committee will exercise control over all Panchayati educational institutions upto upper primary level. Academic supervision of all the schools upto upper primary level, including private schools, will be one of its important functions. The Committee will be responsible for preparation of plans for development of education upto upper primary level in its jurisdiction and for their implementation. It will also prepare educational budget of the Panchayat Samiti and approve expenditure to be incurred. The Committee will coordinate with other bodies for social service programmes for mutual support.

Powers

The Panchayat Samiti Standing Committee on Education will exercise control over the staff in the government schools transferred to Panchayat Samiti including payment of salaries. It will appoint staff to schools under its control from the panel of names given by the appropriate body and transfer them within its jurisdiction subject to guidelines provided by the Zilla Parishad/Government. The Committee will be responsible for channelising grants to aided schools under the supervision of Zilla Parishad. It will have powers of academic supervision of all educational programmes in its jurisdiction upto upper primary level. The Committee will prepare the educational budget and plans of the Panchayat Samiti and sanction expenditure from the approved budget. It may raise its resources by levying development fees and other fees as well as by public contributions and donations. The Committee may propose measures to Panchayat Samiti and Zilla Parishad for mobilisation of additional resources. It may delegate its power of supervision over composite upper primary schools to the Panchayat Standing Committee on Education/Village Education Committee.

Funds

The committee will receive grants from the Zilla Parishad and under various schemes for implementing different educational programmes in its jurisdiction. It may also receive earmarked funds from different agencies, voluntary donations and endowments and may raise funds on its own through the powers of taxation.

Organizational Support

The services of the staff of the education department at this level will be placed with the Panchayat Samiti. However, its control over the staff will be subject to guidelines laid down by the State Government and the academic norms adopted by the Panchayat Samiti Standing Committee on Education will be subject to overall instructions issued by the department of education of the state.

The members of the Panchayati Samiti Standing Committee on Education will require orientation to prepare themselves for the effective discharge of the assigned tasks. They would also require to establish close rapport with officials at different levels and the state-level leadership for guidance in their work. The non-elected members of the Committee also will require orientation to enable them to work in harmony with others. Training for the officials and volunteers for effective implementation of various programmes may also be necessary.

Zilla Parishad Level

According to the Act, the Zilla Parishad will cover an entire district excluding municipal areas.

Zilla Parishad Standing Committee on Education

The Zilla Parishad may set up its Standing Committee on Education as a statutory body under the Panchayati Raj legislation for the management of educational institutions in its jurisdiction. The tenure of the Standing Committee will correspond with the tenure of the Zilla Parishad.

Composition

The Standing Committee may be headed by the Chairman of the Zilla Parishad. The Committee may consist of not less than 15 and not more than 21 members with atleast one-third members being\ women. These should include representatives of Scheduled Cases, Scheduled Tribes, backward classes and minorities. A parent from the Parent-Teacher Associations and one representative each of NGOs and teachers may also be on the Committee. Atleast two representatives of the Education Committee at Panchayat Village level and Panchayat Samiti level may also be nominated to the Committee by rotation. A Principal of a College, a Professor of Eduction of a University or a College teacher, Principal of DIET and Headmaster of a School Complex or Secondary School may also be on the Committee. The Chief Education Officer of the Zilla Parishad may be the Member-Secretary of the Committee. The power of nomination of non-elected members will rest with Zilla Parishad.

Role

The role of the Zilla Parishad Standing Committee on Education will be the overall management and supervision of all educational programmes in the district upto secondary level. The Committee will prepare and implement plans for development of education upto secondary level in the entire district. It will review the progress of education upto secondary level in the district and will also have the specific responsibility for formulation and operationalisation of programmes to achieve total literacy and universal elementary education.

Functions

The Zilla Parishad may establish and manage schools upto secondary level. It will supervise and provide grant to aided schools upto secondary level and will exercise academic supervision of all institutions upto secondary level in the district. Preparation and coordination of plans for development of education upto secondary level may also be the responsibility of this Committee. It will review the progress of education upto secondary level in the district with particular reference to universalisation of elementary education and adult literacy.

One of the important functions of the Committee will be to oversee and guide Panchayat Samiti Standing Committee on Education and Education Committees at Panchayat/Village level in their tasks. The Committee will undertake implementation of academic programmes.

Powers

The powers of the Committee will include establishment and maintenance of schools upto secondary level including recruitment and appointment of staff and payment of salaries, subject to government guidelines. All existing schools upto secondary level will be transferred to the control of Zilla Parishad. In future all secondary schools in the state sector will be established only by the Zilla Parishad. The Committee will also channelise grants to aided schools subject to government rules. It will also exercise academic supervision of all schools including private schools upto secondary level. Laying down academic and administrative norms and procedures under the overall departmental and government supervision may also fall under the purview of the Committee. The Committee will guide the work of Panchayat Samitis and Panchayat/ Village Education Committees. It may recruit and appoint teachers in schools under its control subject to government guidelines. The Committee will also be responsible for preparation of education budget and plans for approval of the Zilla Parishad. The administration of the district education funds will be its responsibility. Preparation of perspective plans for educational development of the district will be the responsibility of the Committee.

Funds

The resources of the Zilla Parishad will include grants from the State Government, the centrally assisted and sponsored schemes channelled through the State Government and funds provided by the other agencies. The Zilla Parished may also raise resources through appropriate taxation measures as well as raise funds through voluntary donations and contributions.

Organizational Support

The services of the staff of the education department at the district level will be placed with the Zilla Parished. The State

Government, particularly the department of education, will provide necessary administrative and academic guidance to the Zilla Parished for undertaking its educational responsibilities.

The Panchayati Raj bodies must take full benefit of the District Institute of Education and Training (DIET) in their efforts to improve the quality of education. The DIET must be fully involved in the functioning of the academic wings of the Panchayati Raj bodies through organisation of orientation and training programmes for the academic staff and by undertaking surveys, evaluation studies and innovative projects. Its supports may also be enlisted for improved methods of learning and assessment procedures for attaining the minimum levels of learning.

Training Needs

The non-officials of the Zilla Parishads would require orientation to introduce them to the tasks of the Zilla Parishad. They may also receive adequate orientation in respect of various schemes in operation as well as programmes, such as, universalisation of elementary education, adult education and non-formal education. The officials working under the Zilla Parished may also require training to enable them to establish effective working relationship with the members of the Committee and Zilla Parishad.

It is now well-recognised that both the non-officials and officials involved in the Panchayati Raj programmes relating to education require orientation, training and preparation for discharging their responsibilities effectively in the new set-up. They need advice, guidance and support to develop sound and efficient methods of functioning in the Panchayati Raj set-up. The state would need to consider setting up appropriate arrangements both at the state and district level to ensure required training and orientation. The establishment of State Institutes of Educational Planning and Administration offers one such possibility.

Personnel Management

Democratic decentralisation implies placing the services of employees with the Panchayati Raj bodies. Therefore, it is necessary to ensure that this is done in a manner and with such safeguards which enable these employees to work in a congenial and cordial atmosphere.

Following this approach, services of the teaching staff working in government primary, middle and secondary schools at the time of transfer to Panchayati Raj Institutions may be placed with the Panchayati Raj bodies. It is necessary to protect their service conditions while doing so. In future all teaching staff in schools under the Panchayati Raj bodies, selected and allotted by an appropriate organisation, will be appointed by the Panchayati Raj bodies and will be under their exclusive control.

All the staff under the Panchayati Raj bodies, whether appointed by them or otherwise, should enjoy the same service conditions and benefits.

The non-teaching staff of the government schools and departmental officers whose services are placed with the Panchayati Raj bodies may be treated on par with similar staff of other departments whose responsibilities and services would stand transferred to the Panchayati Raj bodies.

Educational officers, such as, District Inspectors of Schools, Headmasters of Secondary Schools, District Education Officers and Deputy Directors, who may come under the control of the Panchayati Raj bodies, may be treated as on deputation or on loan of services to these bodies. The Panchayati Raj bodies would have full control over them including disciplines, subject to such guidelines as the state government may lay down.

Recruitment of Teachers

Recruitment of teachers is a sensitive and responsible task. The state government may develop appropriate recruitment system including involvement of the State Public Service Commission wherever necessary. The objective must be to decentralise recruitment of teachers at district level through appropriate bodies with suitable representation of the Zilla Parishad. The procedure must ensure impartial selection through well laid out procedures, with provision for reservation of posts for the prescribed categories. While allocating the candidates to various Panchayat Samitis, it may be ensured that local candidates are preferred. This may minimise the problem of subsequent transfers.

Disbursement of Salaries

The prompt and regular payment of salaries to staff is a matter of importance. The state government must stipulate that the Panchayati Raj bodies introduce mechanisms in their budgetary control to ensure that salary and service benefits flow to the teaching and non-teaching staff in schools in regular and prompt manner.

The state governments may suitably adapt these recommendations to suit the local conditions.

Role of the State Government

While the Panchayati Raj bodies may perform the functions outlined above, the state government or an appropriate state level body would exercise overall supervision and retain residuary powers, particularly in regard to the following issues:

1. Laying down academic standards and norms, including academic calendar, teacher-pupil ratio, etc.
2. Formulation of syllabi and curricula.
3. Preparation and prescription of text-books, supplementary reading materials.
4. Conduct of public, scholarship and other examinations.
5. Teachers' training and retraining.
6. Academic innovations, over-all supervision and assessment.
7. Administrative norms, scale of fees, fee concessions.
8. Norms for transfer of teachers and disciplinary control, etc.
9. Periodic monitoring of the educational activities of the Panchayati Raj bodies and preparation of guidelines for their efficient functioning.
10. Establishment and management of organisations and institutions intended to improve the academic standards and staff development, such as SCERT, SIE, DIETs, etc.

The state and these bodies may consider delegating authority in stages to the Panchayati Raj bodies at different levels for preparation of academic calendar, conduct of examinations, of academic supervision under the over-all guidance of the Department.

Financial Support

Non-Plan Grant

Pending constitution of the State Finance Commission, the grant to Panchayati Raj bodies may include the following non-plan grants:

1. Grant for salary and other benefits to teaching and non-teaching staff. This will include two components:
   (a) The component for the government schools transferred to Zilla Parishad.
   (b) The component for aided schools in the jurisdiction of Zilla Parishad.
2. Maintenance Grant: This may include financial assistance to meet the cost of maintenance of building, equipment, library, contingencies, etc. This may again have two components pertaining to:
   (a) Government schools transferred to Zilla Parishads, and
   (b) Aided schools, as per the norms laid down.

Development Grant (Plan)

This may include:

i) Provision for opening of new schools including salary component for staff.

ii) Provision for construction of building for existing and new schools.

iii) Provision for purchase of equipment and teaching-learning aids for existing and new schools.

iv) Assistance under the centrally sponsored schemes such as Operation Black-board, etc.

v) Assistance under state schemes to schools for improving libraries, science teaching, sports, etc.

vi) Provision for scholarships, fellowships, etc.

The ultimate objective is to transfer all funds which are now operated at district level to the Zilla Parishad for management of education. Notwithstanding the above provisions, the Government will have to equip Zilla Parishads with authority to raise additional resources to support their efforts.

Special Grants

Provision for special grants to Zilla Parishads which are educationally backward will have to be made for reducing disparities.

Incentive Grants

Provision for matching grants for those Zilla Parishads which perform well, according to norms to be laid down, may also need to be made.

Budget

The state budget document should be suitably redesigned to reflect the allocation of funds to Panchayati Raj bodies. The education budget should depict the allocations preferably districtwise under each appropriate head and, if feasible, in accordance with different educational functions assigned to the Panchayati Raj bodies.

Mobilization of Additional Resources

The Zilla Parishad and Panchayat Samiti may suitably be empowered to raise additional resources for educational activities through:

1 Levy of cess on land revenues, sales tax, quarrying, etc.

2. Levy of surcharge on building tax, professional tax, etc.

3. Local contributions towards different schemes for extending benefits to students.

4. Voluntary contributions by parents and community towards supporting development of educational institutions.

The objective must be to encourage the local bodies to generate local resources and supplement the support provided by the state government for undertaking development programmes. The Panchayati Raj bodies should be encouraged to develop cost effective programmes.

Financial Implications

It is an acknowledged fact that resource position of the local bodies is not too happy. Most of them depend upon grants from the state government and other sources. Very few of them have been able to identify and develop sources of income within their own jurisdiction. It is also a fact that by tradition and practice they have not made efforts to generate their resources. Over a period of time they have developed an attitude and approach which essentially implies dependence on outside support. It would therefore be necessary that the Panchayati Raj bodies inculcate a new approach which will favour generation of their own resources and gradual reduction in the dependence on external funding and support. There is also a need for building efficiency and cost effectiveness in their functioning.

These changes, however, can take place only over a period of time. Meanwhile, the transfer of management of education to Panchayati Raj bodies without providing adequate resources to them will be a harmful step. The state government have to ensure sufficient financial support to the Panchayati Raj bodies for ensuring successful management of the educational programmes. Along with the transfer of responsibilities, the funds with which the state government used to discharge such responsibilities, must be made available to the Panchayati Raj bodies.

Special measures are necessary to overcome the acute deficiencies of school infrastructure. The government may, therefore, consider setting up a financial institution exclusively for the development and maintenance of the schools managed by Panchayati Raj and Municipal bodies. This would provide a much needed financial incentive for devolution of powers to these bodies.

Management of Education in Municipal Areas

The Seventy-fourth Amendment Act to the Constitution of India provides for the establishment of the Municipalities in the urban area. It envisages to give the responsibility of "promotion of cultural, educational and aesthetic aspects" to Municipal bodies. The proposals of the Committee in this regard are described in the following paragraphs.

Jurisdiction

The area, population and resources of Municipalities vary significantly from state to state as well as within the State. The responsibilities of educational management to be assigned to the Municipals will have to vary depending upon the specific circumstances of each Municipal body. It is difficult to lay down a broad pattern for this purpose as it has been done in the case of the Panchayati Raj bodies for rural areas. Broadly speaking, the States may categorise the Municipalities according to their jurisdiction, resources and capabilities into three categories. The first category may include Municipalities which may be given the responsibilities of managing education upto primary level, the second category may have responsibilities upto upper primary level, and the third category may be those Municipalities which may be given the control of education upto secondary level.

Structure

The Municipalities may constitute standing committees on education for managing the educational institutions and other responsibilities entrusted to them. These committees may provide for representation of Scheduled Castes, Scheduled Tribes, backward classes and minorities besides elected members of the Municipalities. The parent-teacher association may also be represented on the Committee. Educationists such as a Principal of a college, Headmaster of a secondary school or senior secondary school may also be members of the Committee. Atleast one-third of the members of the committee must be women. The Member-Secretary of the Committee may be the Chief Education Officer of the Municipality or an officer nominated by it. These committees will be responsible for administering the educational programmes in their jurisdiction.

Functions

The government primary, upper primary and secondary schools in the municipal areas along with their staff may be transferred to different Municipalities. They will have control over the staff except in matters of recruitment which will be done by an organisation designated for this purpose by the State Government.

The channelisation of grant to aided schools in the municipal areas may be done through the Municipalities having adequate capabilities to undertake this task.

It is possible that some Municipalities have built up viable management structures which include academic wings. In such cases they may be entrusted with academic supervision of the institutions in the municipal areas subject to guidelines laid down by the Department of Education.

While the Municipalities may prepare plans and programmes for development of educaiton in their jurisdiction, their plans will be coordinated by the District Planning Committee for the district as a whole. The Municipalities will be responsible for promoting universal elementary education and total literacy in their jurisdiction.

The State Government may periodically review the working of the Municipalities in the sphere of education and enlarge their areas of responsibilities with appropriate financial and staff support as they gradually gain experience.

Administrative Support

The staff of the schools transferred to the Municipalities and the headquarter staff provided by the Municipality would provide the administrative support.

Training

Orientation/training may be provided to the members of the Municipal Education Committee and the staff working with them to enable them tc discharge their responsibilities successfully. The

Municipalities may draw upon the resources of DIET to improve the quality of education. The State Government may also organise training programmes in various spheres of educational development for non-official and official members of the Municipalities who are assigned responsibility for education.

Funds

The State Government may provide adequate grants to these bodies for managing the institutions transferred to them. They may also provide development grants for plan programmes in municipal areas. Besides these grants, Municipalities may generate their own resources through appropriate taxation measures.

APPENDIX I

Copy of Government of India, Ministry of Human Resource Development, Department of Education, Order No. F.3-1/93-PN.I, Dated the 2nd February, 1993

The programme of Action, 1992 provides for the setting up of a Central Advisory Board of Education (CABE) Committee on Decentralised Management of Education.

2. The Minister of Human Resource Development, in his capacity as Chairman of the CABE, has, therefore, set up the following Committee:

(i) Shri M. Veerappa Moily — Chairman
Chief Minister
Karnataka

(ii) Dr. (Smt.) Chitra Naik
Member (Education)
Planning Commission

(iii) Shri E.T. Mohammed Basheer
Education Minister
Kerala

(iv) Dr. C. Aranganayagam
Education Minister
Tamil Nadu

(v) Shri S. S. Chakraborty
Education Minister
West Bengal

(vi) Shri Chaitanya Prasad Majhi
Education Minister
Orissa

(vii) Dr. Bhumi Dhar Barman
Education Minister
Assam

(viii) Dr. Karshandas Soneri
Education Minister
Gujarat

(ix) Shri Sudhir Ray, MP
(Member, CABE)

(x) Dr. Syed Hasan
Director
Insan School/College
Kishanganj, Purnea (Bihar)
(Member, CABE)

(xi) Professor Mrinal Miri
Department of Philosophy
N.E.H. University
(Member, CABE)

(xii) Shri P. K. Uma Shankar
Former Director, IIPA
New Delhi
(Chairman, Task Force on
Management of Education)

(xiii) Shri S. R. Sankaran
Former Secretary
Department of Rural Development

(xiv) Shri V.B.L. Mathur
Adviser to Governor of Rajasthan
Jaipur

(xv) Secretary
Department of Legal Affairs

(xvi) Secretary
Department of Rural Development

(xvii) Secretary
Department of Urban Development

(xviii) Dr. R. V. Vaidyanatha Ayyar — Member-Secretary
Joint Secretary
Department of Education
Ministry of Human Resource Development
New Delhi

3. Director (NCERT), Director (NIEPA), Union Education Secretary, Additional Secretary (Education) and Adviser (Education), Planning Commission would be permanent invitees.

4. The terms of reference of the Committee is as under: To formulate guidelines for the management of education on district, sub-district and village levels keeping in view the 72nd and 73rd Amendments to the Constitution of India.

5. The Committee should submit its report within three months of its first meeting.

6. The Committee will lay down its own procedures and methodology of work.

7. The secretarial assistance and other services to the Committee will be provided by the Planning Division of Department of Education

(T.C. James)
Under Secretary to the
Government of India

No. F.3-1/93-PN.I
Government of India
Ministry of Human Resource Development
Department of Education

New Delhi, the 23rd April, 1993

ORDER

***Sub*: CABE Committee on Decentralised Management of Education**

The Minister of Human Resource Development, in his capacity as Chairman of the CABE, has made the following changes in the composition of the CABE Committee on Decentralised Management of Education, constituted *vide* order of even number dated 2nd February, 1993:

(i) Shri Narhari Amin, Education Minister, Gujarat is appointed a member of the Committee *vice* Dr. Karshandas Soneri, former Education Minister, Gujarat.

(ii) Secretary, Ministry of Labour is also appointed a member of the Committee

(T.C. James)
Under Secretary to the
Government of India

New Delhi, the 3rd May 1993

ORDER

***Sub*: CABE Committee on Decentralised Management of Education**

The Minister of Human Resource Development, in his capacity as Chairman of the Central Advisory Board of Education (CABE), has appointed Shri R. D. Sonkar, Adviser in charge of Education, Government of Uttar Pradesh as a member of the

CABE Committee on Decentralised Management of Education constituted vide this Ministry's Order of even number dated the 2nd February, 1993.

(T.C. James)
Under Secretary to the
Government of India

No. F.3-1/93-PN.I
Government of India
Ministry of Human Resource Development
Department of Education

New Delhi, the 30th July, 1993

ORDER

Sub: **CABE Committee on Decentralised Management of Education**

The Minister of Human Resource Development, in his capacity as Chairman of the CABE, has made the following changes in the composition of the CABE Committee on Decentralised Management of Education, constituted *vide* order of even number dated 2nd February, 1993:

(i) Shri G. C. Rajbanshi, Education Minister, Assam is appointed a member of the Committee *vice* Dr. B. D. Barman, former Education Minister, Assam.

(ii) Shri K. Ponnuswamy, Education Minister, Tamil Nadu is also appointed a member of the Committee *vice* former Education Minister, Tamil Nadu, Dr. C. Aranganayagam.

(T.C. James)
Under Secretary to the
Government of India

New Delhi, the 17th August 1993

ORDER

Sub: **CABE Committee on Decentralised Management of Education**

In partial modification of this Office's order of even number dated 2.2.1993, the HRM in his capacity as the Chairman of the CABE has appointed Shri Prafulla Chandra Ghadei, Minister (School Education), Govt. of Orissa as a member of the CABE Committee on Decentralised Management of Education in place of Shri Chaitanya Prasad Majhi, Minister of Higher Education, Govt. of Orissa.

(i) Shri Narhari Amin, Education Minister, Gujarat is appointed a member of the Committee *vice* Dr. Karshandas Soneri, former Education Minister, Gujarat.

(ii) Secretary, Ministry of Labour is also appointed a member of the Committee

(T.C. James)
Under Secretary to the
Government of India

CABE COMMITTEE ON DECENTRALISED MANAGEMENTS OF EDUCATION

Members and Permanent Invitees

Members

1. Shri M. Veerappa Moily — Chairman
   Chief Minister
   Karnataka
2. Dr. (Smt.) Chitra Naik
   Member (Education)
   Planning Commission
   New Delhi
3. Shri E.T. Mohammed Basheer
   Education Minister
   Kerala
4. Professor K. Ponnusamy*
   Education Minister
   Tamil Nadu
5. Shri S.S. Chakraborty
   Education Minister
   West Bengal
6. Shri Prafulla Chandra Ghadai**
   Education Minister
   Orissa
7. Sri G. C. Rajbanshi***
   Education Minister
   Assam
8. Shri Narhari Amin****
   Education Minister
   Gujarat
9. Dr. Sudhir Ray, MP
   (Member, CABE)
10. Dr. Syed Hasan
    Director, Insan School/College
    Kishanganj, Purnea (Bihar)
    (Member, CABE)

11. Professor Mrinal Miri
Department of Philosophy
North Eastern Hill University, Shillong
(Member, CABE)

12. Shri P. K. Uma Shankar
Formar Director, IIPA
New Delhi
(Chairman, Task Force on Management of Education)

13. Shri S. R. Sankaran
Former Secretary
Department of Rural Development

14. Shri V. B. L. Mathur
Adviser to Governor of Rajasthan
Jaipur

15. Shri R. D. Sonkar
Adviser to Governor of Uttar Pradesh
Lucknow

16. Secretary
Department of Legal Affairs
Ministry of Law, Justice
and Company Affairs
New Delhi

17. Secretary
Ministry of Rural Development
New Delhi

18. Secretary
Ministry of Urban Development
New Delhi

19. Secretary
Ministry of Labour
New Delhi

20. Dr. R. V. Vaidyanatha Ayyar — Member-Secretary
Joint Secretary
Department of Education
Ministry of Human Resource Development
New Delhi

Permanent Invitees

1. Dr. P. V. Ranga Rao
   Education Minister
   Andhra Pradesh

2. Secretary
   Department of Education
   Ministry of Human Resource Development
   New Delhi

3. Additional Secretary
   Department of Education
   Ministry of Human Resource Development
   New Delhi.

4. Adviser (Education)
   Planning Commission
   New Delhi

5. Director
   National Council of Educational
   Research and Training
   New Delhi

6. Joint Director
   National Institute of Educational
   Planning and Administration
   New Delhi

7. Dr. S. C. Nuna
   Fellow
   National Institute of Educational
   Planning and Administration
   New Delhi

* In place of Dr. C. Arranganayagam w.e.f. 30th July, 1993.

** In place of Shri Chaitanya Prasad Majhi w.e.f. 17th August, 1993.

*** In place of Dr. Karshandas Soneri w.e.f. 23rd April, 1993.

**** In place of Dr. Bhumi Dhar Barman w.e.f. 30th July, 1993.

APPENDIX II

List of Documents Circulated to The Members of the CABE Committee on Decentralised Management of Education

Basic Texts

B.1 The Constitution (Seventy-Second Amendment) Bill, 1991.

B.2 The Constitution (Seventy-Third Amendment) Bill, 1991.

B.3 *National Policy on Education 1986,* (Revised 1992).

B.4 *Programme of Action (1992),* Chapter on "Management of Education".

C Series: Documents prepared by the Core Group

C.1 Panchayati Raj bodies and Development: A Perspective.

C.2 Experience of Panchayati Raj bodies in the field of Education in the States of Andhra Pradesh, Gujarat, Karnataka, Maharashtra and Uttar Pradesh.

C.3 Issues to be considered by the CABE Committee while formulating its Recommendation on the Decentralised Management of Education under the Panchayati Raj Institutions.

C.4 Structure, Role and Functions of Panchayati Raj Institutions in Andhra Pradesh

C.5 Structure, Role and Functions of Panchayati Raj Institutions of Gujarat.

C.6 Structure, Role and Functions of Panchayati Raj Institutions in Karnataka.

C.7 Structure, Role and Functions of Panchayati Raj Institutions in Maharashtra.

D Series: Documents of the Ministry of Human Resource Development, Department of Education

D.1 National Policy on Education, 1986-Implementation Strategies (A draft working paper for the previous CABE Committee on Management of Education).

D.2 Report of the Sub-Committee of the CABE Committee on Management of Education.

D.3 Decentralisation and Participative Management (A paper submitted to the CABE Committee on Policy by the Department of Education).

N Series: Documents published by the National Institute of Rural Development, Hyderabad, on Panchayati Raj

N.1 *Summary of Major Reports on Panchayati Raj*

N.2 *Salient Features of Panchayati Raj Acts*

N.3 *Structural Patterns*

P Series: Papers on Decentralised Management of Education in some Countries

P.1 Towards Conformity: Educational Control and the Growth of Corporate Management in England and France by *Patricia Broadfoot.*

P.2 Finance as a Means of Control in English Education: Recent Trends Towards Centralisation by *Alan Crispin.*

P.3 Educational Change and the Control Question: Scandinvian Perspectives by *Jon Lauglo.*

P.4 Decentralisation and Equality of Educational Opportunity in Papua New Guinea by *Mark Brag.*

P.5 Decentralisation of Education in Northern Nigeria: A Case of Continuing 'Indirect Rule'? by *David Stephens.*

S Series: Comments of State Governments/UTs Administration in response to Chairman's Communication

S.1 Comments of Government of Andhra Pradesh

S.2 Comments of Administration of Chandigarh

S.3 Comments of Administration of Daman and Diu

S.4 Comments of Administration of Dadara and Nagar Haveli

S.5 Comments of Government of Goa

S.6 Comments of Government of Gujarat

S.7 Comments of Government of Himachal Pradesh

S.8 Comments of Government of Jammu and Kashmir

S.9 Comments of Government of Karnataka

S.10 Comments of Government of Maharashtra

S.11 Comments of Government of Orissa

S.12 Comments of Administration of Pondicherry

S.13 Comments of Government of Punjab

S.14 Comments of Government of Rajasthan

S.15 Comments of Government of Sikkim

S.16 Comments of Government of Uttar Pradesh

OD Series: Other Documents

OD.1 "Power to the People", Speech of the Late Prime Minister

OD.2 Suggestions of Syed Shahabuddin, M.P. for the Consideration of the Committee

OD.3 *The Orissa Education Act, 1969*

OD.4 *The Government of Goa, Daman and Diu Education Act, 1984*

APPENDIX III

National Policy on Education (Revised 1992)

(EXTRACTS)

Part X
THE MANAGEMENT OF EDUCATION

An overhaul of the system of planning and the management of education will receive high priority. The guiding considerations will be:

a) Evolving a long-term planning and management perspective of education and its integration with the country's developmental and manpower needs;

b) Decentralisation and the creation of a spirit of autonomy for educational institutions;

c) Giving pre-eminence to people's involvement, including association of non-govenmental agencies and voluntary effort;

d) Inducting more women in the planning and management of education;

e) Establishing the principle of accountability in relation to given objectives and norms.

National Level

The Central Advisory Board of Education will play a pivotal role in reviewing educational development, determining the changes required to imprcve the system and monitoring implementation. It will function through appropriate Committees and other mechanisms created to ensure contact with, and coordination among, the various areas of Human Resource Development. The Departments of Education at the Centre and in the State will be strengthened through the involvement of professionals.

Indian Education Service

A proper management structure in education will entail the establishment of the Indian Education Service as an All-India Service. It will bring a national perspective to this vital sector. The basic principles, functions and procedures of recruitment to this service will be decided in consultation with the State Governments.

State Level

State Governments may establish State Advisory Boards of Education on the lines of CABE. Effective measures should be taken to integrate mechanism in the various State departments concerned with Human Resource Development.

Special attention will be paid to the training of educational planners, administrators and heads of institutions. Institutional arrangements for this purpose should be set up in stages.

District and Local Level

District Boards of Education will be created to manage education upto the higher secondary level. State Governments will attend to this aspect with all possible expedition. Within a multi-level framework of educational development, Central, State and District and Local level agencies will participate in planning, coordination, monitoring and evaluation.

A very important role must be assigned to the head of an educational institution. Heads will be specially selected and trained. School complexes will be promoted on a flexible pattern so as to serve as networks of institutions and synergic alliances to encourage professionalism among teachers, to ensure observance of norms of conduct and to enable the sharing of experiences and facilities. It is expected that a developed system of school complexes will take over much of the inspection functions in due course.

Local communities, through appropriate bodies, will be assigned a major role in programmes of school improvement.

Voluntary Agencies and Aided Institutions

Non-government and voluntary effort including social activist groups will be encouraged, subject to proper management, and financial assistance provided. At the same time, steps will be taken to prevent the establishment of institutions set up to commercialise education.

Redress of Grievances

Educational tribunals, fashioned after Administrative Tribunals, will be established at the national and state levels.

APPENDIX IV

PROGRAMME OF ACTION (1992)

23. THE MANAGEMENT OF EDUCATION
(EXTRACTS)

1. Educational Management System

The National Policy on Education (NPE) is comprehensive and envisages wide-ranging action on a variety of issues and problems. Yet it seeks a convergence of such action to secure a total and coordinated impact. It also reaches beyond the education sector to link effectively with other sectors of social development to achieve quick and positive results.

The task of ensuring effective implementation of the NPE rests on the education management system. Flexible and relevant management structures and organisations, processes and procedures are needed all along the line to secure the detailed planning and implementation of the Programme of Action (POA).

Education in India has been largely a budget-based system where efficiency is rated by ability to "consume" budget and to demand more. Performance at delivery point has not been an important criterion. The on-going economic reforms and structural adjustments would, therefore, demand a shift from inputs to performance and outcomes-consideration of cost effectiveness should inform all levels of educational administration and planning.

Absence of effective decentralisation, failure to evolve priorities and pursue objective-oriented programmes, weak personnel management system, and ineffective intra-departmental and inter-departmental coordinating mechanisms have adversely affected the performance of the education system. Even routine tasks like the supply of text-books, conduct of examinations and operation of academic calendar are not being properly attended to. The highest priority in POA should be to ensure that these routine tasks are performed properly and that the delivery of education services improves at all levels.

Soon after adoption of POA 1986, the Central Advisory Board of Education (CABE) had constituted committees to recommend measures for toning up educational management. These committees prepared draft reports for pursuing action with the states and other authorities concerned. However, due to frequent political changes, action could not be pursued on many of these initiatives. It is now necessary to resume action and pursue these objectives vigorously.

This chapter covers only management issues which cover the entire field of education and those which cover more than one sub-sector of education.

2. Decentralisation and Involvement of People

The NPE and POA have emphasised the importance of decentralising planning and management of education at all levels and involving people in the process. Decentralisation implies democratic participation by elected representatives of people in decision-making at the district, sub-district and Panchayat levels. In pursuance of the POA provision the State Governments have been taking steps to set up structures for decentralised planning and management. The future course of decentralisation would be influenced to a great extent by the proposed Constitution Amendment (Seventy-second) Bill, 1991; they would have to be finalised after the Bill is enacted.

3. (a) The Constitution (Seventy-second) Amendment Bill 1991

The Constitution (Seventy-second) Amendment Bill of 1991 on Panchayati Raj institutions envisages introduction of democratically elected bodies at the district, sub-district and panchyat levels. These bodies will be responsible for the preparation of plans for the economic development and social justice. The Bill provides for representation of women, scheduled castes and scheduled tribes.

The proposed Eleventh Schedule of the Constitution provides, among other things, for entrusting to Panchayati Raj bodies of:

"Education including primary and secondary schools, technical training and vocational education, adult and non-formal education, libraries, and cultural activities".

The subjects closely allied to education, namely, health, welfare, women and child development are also to be entrusted to the Panchayati Raj bodies.

(b) State Legislation

The Panchayati Raj Bill is an enabling legislation. The states are to frame their own legislation in their turn. The states would need to draw up appropriate legislations which, among other things, must provide for Panchayati Raj Committees for Education.

(c) District Level Body

Within this legislation a district-level body may be set up with the responsibility for implementation of all educational programmes including non-formal and adult education, and school education up to the higher secondary level. The district body will provide for representation of educationists, women, youth, representatives of parents, scheduled castes/scheduled tribes, minorities and appropriate institutions in the district. Representation may also be provided for urban bodies and cantonments which organise educational activities. The district body will also be vested with the responsibility for planning which would include, inter alia, area development, spatial planning, institutional planning, administrative and financial control and personnel management with respect to primary middle, secondary and higher secondary schools and other educational programmes. Implementation of different educational programmes at the district level will be supervised and monitored by the body. The district educational plans will also go into the levels of participation and retention of boys and girls under different age-groups by socio-cultural and economic categories, particularly SC & ST, and plan for measures for ensuring physical infrastructure, equitable access as well as qualitative aspects of education.

In order that the district body discharges the functions allotted, it would be necessary to assign state funds for implementation of the various programmes. Provision will also be made to enable the district body to raise its own resources. Funds, which are not earmarked, will also be placed at its disposal so that these resources can be used for any purpose that may be considered essential by raising matching funds of its own.

The relationship of the State Government with the district level body in terms of administrative and financial control and personnel management will be clearly spelt out in appropriate guidelines to be issued by the State Governments. It will also be necessary to clarify the levels of recruitment and structure of cadres of teachers of different categories.

There will be a Chief Education Officer for the District to look after all levels of schools, adult and non-formal education. Under him, there will be a District Education Officer looking after establishment, budgeting, planning and the educational data base. In addition, there will be district-level officials of appropriate rank engaged in specific educational programmes. The Chief Education Officer will be he principal education officer of the district body.

The district body will draw upon the expertise of the District Institute of Education and Training (DIET), and other institutions for substantive curricular and pedagogic inputs into all programmes of elementary education, non-formal education and adult education at the district level. It may also seek the support of institutions of higher education in the district.

In states and areas where the Constitution (Seventy-second) Amendment Bill, 1991 will not apply, such bodies on similar lines may be set up at district level.

(d) Village Education Committee

Under the Constitution Amendment Bill, Panchayats will be formed for a village or a group of villages. The Panchayat will have elected representatives. Besides, each Panchayat may constitute a Village Education Committee (VEC) which would be responsible for administration of the delegated programmes in the field of education at the village level. The major responsibility of the VECs should be operationalisation of micro-level planning and school mapping in the village through systematic house to house survey and periodic discussion with the parents. It should be the endeavour of the committee that every child in every family participates in the primary education. In these activities they will be provided expert guidance and support by DIET.

The State Governments may consider entrusting the following functions to the VEC:

Generation and sustenance of awareness among the village community ensuring participation of all segments of population; and

Developing teacher/instructor and community partnership to oversee and manage the effective and regular functioning of the schools and centres.

In view of the critical role and function of VEC, it should be vested with appropriate statutory and necessary financial and administrative authority.

(e) Model Legislation

It would be necessary for the Ministry of Human Resource Development (MHRD) to prepare, models statutory provisions for the guidance of states when they formulate their legislation under the Panchayati Raj Act. As other sectors such as health, women and child development, social welfare are also involved, MHRD may also consider preparing comprehensive model legislation covering all these areas for achieving coordination. This may be done in collaboration with the concerned Central Ministries/Departments and Planning Commission. The preparation of this model Bill may commence immediately as it will be required by the States when the Constitution Amendment Bill is brought into effect.

(f) Urban Local Bodies

The Constitution Amendment Bill on Urban Local Bodies provides for constitution of Municipal Corporations, Municipal

Councils and Nagar Panchayats. The proposed Twelfth Schedule to the Constitution provides for entrusting these bodies with "promotion of cultural, educational and aesthetic aspects". These bodies would be entrusted with appropriate statutory responsibilities with regard to the education sector by an appropriate state legislation. The MHRD may prepare model legislation in this area also for the consideration of the states.

4. Involvement of Voluntary and Non-governmental Agencies

The successful implementation of programmes like elementary education including non-formal education, early child-hood care and education, adult education, education of the disabled, etc. will require people's involvement at the grass-root level and participation of voluntary agencies and social activist groups on a much larger scale. Considering the need for ensuring relationship of genuine partnership between the government and voluntary agencies, the government will take positive steps to promote their wider involvement. Consultations will be held with them from time to time about programmes and procedures for selection of voluntary and non-governmental agencies. The procedures for financial assistance will be streamlined to enable them to play optimal role.

It would be desirable for the state governments to develop specific action plan for entrusting selected programmes of educational development to voluntary agencies and non-governmental oranisations. They could be used to supplement effectively the on-going programmes to enhance their quality and impact. They should be allowed to function in a congenial and supportive atmosphere. It is expected that appropriate indices of accountability in terms of performance would be evolved in consultation with the voluntary organisations and NGOs.

5. Accountability and Efficiency

Norms of performance by the different categories of educational personnel and institutions must be prepared by the states. The MHRD may assist them in the preparation of such norms. These should be finalised after due consultation and discussions with the representative groups. Norms which are finalised must be given publicity and the performance should be duly notified. Non-observance of norms must result in disincentives while good performance must receive recognition, incentives and due publicity.

Monitoring of all educational programmes for implementation at the district will take place at the state level and relevant indicators for inter-district comparison will need to be worked out. Suitable incentives may be provided to the districts linked to their achievements. Similar arrangements may be developed for the Block and Panchayat level institutions.

In view of the constraint of resources, cost effectiveness has to be promoted in educational planning and administration at all levels. Financial and administrative norms relating to the educational programmes will need to be evolved and enforced with greater diligence. Mere budgetary concern must be replaced by assessment of efficiency on the basis of carefully developed indices of educational and institutional achievements. Location and establishment of institutions should be planned rationally with due regard to the catchment areas of existing institutions, identification of unserved and underserved areas, and the possibility of expanding facilities in existing institutions. As far as possible facilities should be shared among institutions and extrashifts resorted to in urban areas to provide better utilisation of resources. The chapters on Higher Education and Technical Education (chapter 11 and 15) have spelt out some measures in this regard.

All procedures and processes which hamper the functioning of institutions and hold up programme implementation must be reviewed and simplified. For example, migration, conduct and identification certificates and similar other plethora of outmoded practices only hinder programmes of education. Simplified manual of instructions and codes must be evolved to facilitate the proposed reforms in education. Modernisation of educational offices will enhance their efficiency.

6. Strengthening of Educational Planning and Administration

(a) School and Educational Complexes

School complexes will be promoted as a network of institutions on a flexible pattern to provide synergic alliances to encourage professionalism among teachers, to ensure observance of norms and conduct and to enable the sharing of experiences and facilities. The school complex will serve as the lowest viable unit of area planning and will form a cluster of 8-10 institutions in which different institutions can reinforce each other by exchanging resources, personnel, materials, teaching aids, etc. and using them on a sharing basis.

It is expected that in course of time, school complexes when fully developed, will take over much of the inspection functions including educational mapping, grading of institutions and identifying strength and weakness of individual schools. Inspection to be conducted will invoke a culture of participation and providing corrective rather than the existing practice of finding faults. These inspections will be in addition to the normal routine inspection functions of district/block level inspecting authorities.

Guidelines for functioning of school complexes have been prepared and communicated to the State governments. Although a number of states have experimented with the scheme of school complexes, the programme is yet to emerge as a comprehensive and systematically administered one. As the institutional resource endowment varies from place to place, there can be no single model for creation of school complexes. Every state has to evolve its own operational model based on its experiences or by drawing upon experiences of other states. The states may prescribe necessary guidelines for creation and functioning of school complexes and define the nature, mode, type of planning and inspection work to be performed by them. Considering that some of the schools forming part of the complex will be non-government institutions, the State governments may give them necessary assistance to facilitate their participation. It would be desirable that the recommendations regarding the schools complex programme are implemented on a state-wise basis during the Eighth Plan period.

At the same time it is desirable to attempt larger networking of institutions in a district in the shape of educational complexes on an experimental basis during the Eighth Plan period. In the educational complex, the networking could be done from the primary to college and university level. The Central Government may develop in the next two years guidelines for organising this on an experimental basis in situations where the atmosphere is congenial for launching such complexes. While developing the educational complexs, support from institutions like DIET, Teacher Education Colleges, ITIs, Polyechnics, particularly Community Polytechnics may also be sought.

(b) Block Level Administration

It is observed that the block-level set up of educational administration is very weak almost all over the country. The supervisors often have little contact with the schools. The routine administrative duties such as collecting statistic, disbursement of salaries, posting and transfers of the staff take up most of their time. The following steps may be taken to improve the functioning of block-level education set up:

(i) Norms, not only on the basis of number of schools but also number of teachers should be evolved through systematic studies so that the block-level education officer may effectively cope with his administrative responsibilities and supervisory functions.

(ii) Most of the time of block-level eduction officers is spent on routine administrative work. Their duties may be laid down in detail so that their support for the academic programmes gets due importance.

(c) District Educational Administration

The jurisdiction of a district for the educational purpose may be co-terminus with its revenue jurisdiction. The big districts could be divided into sub-educational districts but these will be coordinated and controlled by a Chief Education Officer (CEO) for the whole district. He will look after all levels of education—primary, middle secondary and higher secondary, non-formal and adult education. The planning and statistics branch of CEO will by provided with computer facilities for Educational Management Information System (EMIS).

For purposes of academic inspections, district supervisors of education may be provided on the basis of number of schools to be looked after for academic supervision. In discharge of these functions, the supervisors will also coordinate their activities with District Institutes of Education and Training.

(d) State Level Administration

In most states there are a number of directors and secretaries to take care of various sectors of education. In most of the cases this expansion is taking place by re-organisation of existing positions. States may consider reorganising their educational administrative set-up at various levels and strengthen it on the basis of certain norms which could be evolved for this purpose.

With the increase in number of departments/directorates dealing with education, states may have to evolve appropriate mechanism for their coordination. In most States, Directorates and Secretariat Departments dealing with the education have proliferated as a result of expansion of institutions and programmes. The need for appropriate mechanisms for coordination of this multiple organisation operating in the same area is acutely felt. The delivery of education services and programmes is also being impaired by the absence of proper linkages between education and other areas of Human Resource Development (HRD). Many possibilities exist. One possibility could be separate Director-General of Education to coordinate the activities of various Directorates. Another could be for a Principal Secretary or Additional Chief Secretary to coordinate the various Departments of Education in the Secretariat. In case of states having more than one Minister dealing with education, there is a need for setting up of a Cabinet Committee which could coordinate and monitor educational programmes. Similar mechanism can also be envisaged for overall coordination in different areas of HRD. It seems appropriate to designate an Additional Chief Secretary to coordinate the activities of different sectors related to Human Resource Development–a HRD Commissioner on the lines of the Agricultural Production Commissioner.

Similar arrangements may be attempted to secure over-all coordination in human resource development. In case of states having more than one minister dealing with education, there is a need for setting up of a Cabinet Committee which could coordinate and monitor educational programmes.

(e) State Advisory Boards of Education

The NPE envisaged that the state governments would establish State Boards of Education (SABE) on the lines of CABE. The SABE will function as an apex body to coordinate all human resource development programmes. On the basis of available information, it seems that the Boards have not been set up in most of the states. The need for coordinated approach to educational policy and planning at the state level cannot be cannot be exaggerated and the states will be advised to set up SABEs preferably before 1995.

The composition of the SABE may follow the pattern of CABE. There may be institutional and organisational representatives besides eminent educationists and experts. Representations of weaker section of society particularly women, SC/ST and minority community should be ensured.

APPENDIX V

THE CONSTITUTION (SEVENTY-THIRD AMENDMENT) ACT, 1992

AN ACT

further to amend the Constitution of India

BE it enacted by Parliament in the Forty-third year of the Republic of India as follows:—

Short title and commencement. 1. (1) This Act may be called the Constitution (Seventy-third Amendment) Act, 1992).

(2) It shall come into force on such date as the Central Government may, by notification in the Official Gazette, appoint.

Insertion of new Part IX. 2. After Part VIII of the Constitution, the following Part shall be inserted, namely:—

PART IX

THE PANCHAYATS

Definitions. 243. In this Part, unless the context otherwise requires—

(a) "district" means a district in a State:

(b) "Gram Sabha" means a body consisting of persons registered in the electoral rolls relating to a village comprised within the area of Panchayat at the village level;

(c) "Intermediate level" means a level

between the village and district levels specified by the Governor of a State by public notification to be the intermediate level for the purposes of this Part;

(d) "Panchayat" means an institution (by whatever name called) of self-government constituted under article, 243B, for the rural areas;

(e) "Panchayat area" means the territorial area of a Panchayat;

(f) "Panchayat" means the population as ascertained at the last preceding census of which the relevant figures have been published;

(g) "village" means a village specified by the Governor by public notification to be a village for the purposes of this Part and includes a group of villages so specified.

Gram Sabha.

243A. A Gram Sabha may exercise such powers and perform such functions at the village level as the Legislature of State may by law, provide.

Constitution of Panchayats.

243B. (1) There shall be constituted in every State, Panchayats at the village, intermediate and district levels in accordance with the provisions of this Part.

(2) Notwithstanding anything in clause (1), Panchayats at the intermediate level may not be constituted in a State having a population not exceeding twenty lakhs.

Composition of Panchayats.

243C. (1) Subject to the provisions of this Part, the Legislature of a State may, by law, make provisions with respect to the composition of Panchayats.

Provided that the ratio between the population of the territorial area of a Panchayat at any level and the number of seats in such

Panchayat to be filled by election shall, so far as practicable, be the same throughout the State.

(2) All the seats in a Panchayat shall be filled by persons chosen by direct election from territorial constituencies in the Panchayat area and; for this purpose, each Panchayat area shall be divided into territorial constituencies in such manner that the ratio between the population of each constituency and the number of seats allotted to it shall, so far as practicable, be the same throughout the Panchayat area.

(3) The Legislature of a State may, by law, provide for the representation—

(a) of the Chairpersons of the Panchayats at the village level, in the Panchayats at the intermediate level or, in the case of a State not having Panchayats at the intermediate level, in the Panchayats at the district level;

(b) of the Chairpersons of the Panchayats at the intermediate level, in the Panchayats at the district level.

(c) of the members of the House of the People and the members of the Legislative Assembly of the State representing constituencies which comprise wholly or partly a Panchayat area at a level other than the village level, in such Panchayat;

(d) of the member of the Council of States and the members of the Legislative Council of the State, where they are registered as electors within—

(i) a Panchayat area at the intermediate level in Panchayat at the intermediate level;

(ii) a Panchayat area at the district level, in Panchayat at the district level;

(4) The Chairperson of a Panchayat and other members of a Panchayat whether or not chosen by direct election from territorial constituencies in the Panchayat area shall have the right to vote in the meeting of the Panchayats.

(5) The Chairperson of—

(a) a Panchayat at the village level shall be elected in such manner as the Legislature of a State may, by law, provide; and

(b) a Panchayat at the intermediate level or district level shall be elected by, and from amongst, the elected members thereof.

Reservation of Seats.

243D. (1) Seats shall be reserved for—

(a) the Schedule Castes; and

(b) the Scheduled Tribes,

in every Panchayat and the number of seats so reserved shall bear, as may be, the same proportion to the total number of seats to be filled by direct election in that Panchayat as the population of the Scheduled Castes in that Panchayat area or of the Scheduled Tribes in that Panchayat area bears to the total population of that area and such seats may be allotted by rotation to different constituencies in a Panchayat.

(2) Not less than one-third of the total number of seats reserved under clause (1) shall be reserved for women belonging to the Scheduled Castes or, as the case may be, the Scheduled Tribes.

(3) Not less than on-third (including the number of seats reserved for women belonging to the Scheduled Castes and the Scheduled Tribes) of the total number of seats to be filled by direct election in every Panchayat shall be

reserved for women and such seats may be allotted by rotation to different constituencies in a Panchayat.

(4) The offices of the Chairpersons in the Panchayats at the village or any other level shall be reserved for the Scheduled Castes, the Scheduled Tribes and women in such manner as the Legislature of a State may, by law, provide:

Provided that the number of offices of Chairpersons reserved for the Scheduled Castes and the Scheduled Tribes in the Panchayats at each level in any State shall bear, as nearly as may be, the same proportion to the total number of such offices in the Panchayats at each level as the population of the Scheduled Caste in the State or of the Scheduled Tribes in the State bears to the total population of the State:

Provided further that not less than one-their of the total number of offices of Chairpersons in the Panchayats at each level shall be reserved for women:

Provided also that the number of offices reserved under this clause shall be allotted by rotation to different Panchayats at each level.

(5) The reservation of seats under clauses (1) and (2) and the reservation of offices of Chairpersons (other than the reservation for women) under clause (4) shall cease to have effect on the expiration of the period specified in article 334.

(6) Nothing in this Part shall prevent the Legislature of a State from making any provision for reservation of seats in any Panchayat or offices of Chairpersons in the Panchayats at any level in favour of backward class of citizens.

Duration of Panchayats etc.

243E. (1) Every Panchayat, unless sooner dissolved under any law for the time being in force, shall continue for five years from the date appointed for its first meeting and no longer.

(2) No amendment, of any law for the time being in force shall have the effect of causing dissolution of a Panchayat at any level, which is functioning immediately before such amendment till the expiration of its duration specified in clause (1).

(3) An election to constitute a Panchayat shall be completed—

(a) before the expiry of its duration specified in clause (1);

(b) before the expiration of a period of six months from the date of its dissolution:

Provided that where the remainder of the period for which the dissolved Panchayat would have continued is less than six months, it shall not be necessary to hold any election under this clause for constituting the Panchayat for such period.

(4) A Panchayat constituted upon the dissolution of a Panchayat before the expiration of its duration shall continue only for the remainder of the period for which the dissolved Panchayat would have continued under clause (1) had it not been so dissolved.

Disqualifications for membership.

243F. (1) A person shall be disqualified for being chosen as, and for being, a member of a Panchayat—

(a) if he is so disqualified by or under any law for the time being in force for the purposes of elections to the legislature of the State concerned:

Provided that no person shall be disqualified on the ground that he is less than twenty-five years of age, if he has attained the age of twenty-one years;

(b) if he is so disqualified by or under any law made by the Legislature of the State.

(2) If any question arises as to whether a member of a Panchayat has become subject to any of the disqualifications mentioned in clause (1), the question shall be referred for the decision of such authority and in such manner as the Legislature of a State may, by law, provide.

Powers, authority and responsibilities of Panchayats.

243G. Subject to the provisions of this Constitution, the Legislature of a State may, by law, endow the Panchayats with such powers and authority as may be necessary to enable them to function as institutions of self-government and such law may contain provisions for the devolution of powers and responsibilities upon Panchayats at the appropriate level, subject to such conditions as may be specified therein, with respect to—

(a) the preparation of plans for economic development and social justice;

(b) the implementation of schemes for economic development and social justice as may be entrusted to them including those in relation to the matters listed in the Eleventh Schedule.

Powers to impose taxes by, and Funds of, the Panchayats.

243H. The Legislature of a State may, by law—

(a) authorise a Panchayat to levy, collect and appropriate such taxes, duties, tolls and fees in accordance with such procedure and subject to such limits;

(b) assign to a Panchayat such taxes, duties, tolls and fees levied and collected by the State Government for such purposes and subject to such conditions and limits;

(c) provide for making such grants-in-aid to the Panchayats from the Consolidated Fund of the State; and

(d) provide for constitution of such Funds for crediting all moneys received, respectively, by or on behalf of the Panchayats and also for the withdrawal of such moneys therefrom.

as may be specified in the law.

Constitution of Finance Commission to review financial position.

243-I. (1) The Governor of a State shall, as soon as may be within one year from the commencement of the Constitution (Seventy-third Amendment) Act, 1992, and thereafter at the expiration of every fifth year, constitute a Finance Commission to review the financial position of the Panchayats and to make recommendations to the Governor as to—

(a) the principles which should govern—

(i) the distribution between the State and the Panchayats of the net proceeds of the taxes, duties, tolls and fees leviable by the State, which may be divided between them under this Part and the allocation between the Panchayats at all levels of their respective shares of such proceeds;

(ii) the determination of the taxes, duties, tolls and fees which may be assigned to, or appropriated by, the Panchayats;

(iii) the grant-in-aid to the Panchayats from the Consolidated Fund of the State;

(b) the measures needed to improve the financial position of the Panchayats;

(c) any other matter referred to the Finance Commission by the Governor in the interests of sound finance of the Panchayats.

(2) The Legislature of a State may, by law, provide for the composition of the Commission, the qualifications which shall be requisite for appointment as members thereof and the manner in which they shall be selected.

(3) The Commission shall determine their procedure and shall have such powers in the performance of their functions as the Legislature of the State may, by law, confer on them.

(4) The Governor shall cause every recommendation made by the Commission under this article together with an explanatory memorandum as to the action taken thereon to be laid before the Legislature of the State.

Audit of accounts of Panchayats.

243J. The Legislature of a State may, by law, make provisions with respect to the maintenance of accounts by the Panchayats and the auditing of such accounts.

Elections to the Panchayats.

243K. (1) The superintendence, direction and control of the preparation of electoral rolls for, and the conduct of, all elections to the Panchayats shall be vested in a State Election Commission consisting of a State Election Commissioner to be appointed by the Governor.

(2) Subject to the provisions of any law made by the Legislature of a State, the conditions of service and tenure of office of the State Election Commissioner shall be such as the Governor may by rule determine:

Provided that the State Election Commissioner shall not be removed from his office except in like manner and on the like grounds as a Judge of a High Court and the conditions of service of the State Election Commissioner shall not be varied to his disadvantage after his appointment.

(3) The Governor of a State shall, when so requested by the State Election Commission, make available to the State Election Commission such staff as may be necessary for the discharge of the functions conferred on the State Election Commission by clause (1).

(4) Subject to the provisions of this Constitution the Legislature of a State may, by Law, make provision with respect to all matters relating to, or in connection with, elections to the Panchayats.

Application to Union territories. 243L. The provisions of this Part shall apply to the Union territories and shall in their application to a Union territory, have effect as if the references to the Governor of a State were references to the Administrator of the Union territory appointed under article 239 and references to the Legislature or the Legislative Assembly of a State were references, in relation to a Union territory having a Legislative Assembly, to that Legislative Assembly:

Provided that the President may, by public notification, direct that the provisions of this Part shall apply to any Union territory or part thereof subject to such exceptions and modifications as he may specify in the notification.

Part not to apply to certain areas. 243M. (1) Nothing in this Part shall apply to the Scheduled Areas referred to in clause (1), and the tribal areas referred to in clause (2), of article 244.

(2) Nothing in this Part shall apply to—

(a) the States of Nagaland, Meghalaya and Mizoram;

(b) the hill areas in the State of Manipur for which District Councils exist under any law for the time being in force.

(3) Nothing in this Part—

(a) relating to Panchayats at the district level shall apply to the hill areas of the District of Darjeeling in the state of West Bengal for which Darjeeling Gorkha Hill Council exists under any law for the time being in force;

(b) shall be construed to affect the functions and powers of the Darjeeling Gorkha Hill Council constituted under such law.

(4) Notwithstanding anything in this Constitution—

(a) the Legislature of a State referred to in sub-clause (a) of clause (2) may, by law, extend this Part to that State, except the areas, if any, referred to in clause (1), if the Legislative Assembly of that State passes a resolution to that effect by a majority of the total membership of that House and by a majority of not less than two-thirds of the members of that House present and voting:

(b) Parliament may, by law, extend the provisions of this Part to the Scheduled Areas and the tribal areas referred to in clause (1) subject to such exceptions and modifications as may be specified in such law, and no such law shall be deemed to be an amendment of this Constitution for the purposes of article 368.

Continuance of existing laws and Panchayats.

243N. Notwithstanding anything in this Part, any provision of any law relating to Panchayats in force in a State immediately before the commencement of the Constitution (Seventy-third Amendment) Act, 1992, which is inconsistent with the provisions of this Part, shall continue to be in force until amended or repealed by a competent Legislature or other competent authority or until the expiration of one year from such commencement, whichever is earlier.

Provided that all the Panchayats existing immediately before such commencement shall continue till the expiration of their duration, unless sooner dissolved by a resolution passed to the effect by the Legislative Assembly of that State or, in the case of a State having a Legislative Council, by each House of the Legislature of that State.

Bar to interference by courts in electoral matters.

243O. Notwithstanding anything in this Constitution—

(a) the validity of any law relating to the delimitation of constituencies or the allotment of seats to such constituencies made or purporting to be made under article 243K, shall not be called in question in any court;

(b) no election to any Panchayat shall be called in question except by an election petition presented to such authority and in such manner as is provided for by or under any law made by the Legislature of a State.

Amendment of article 280.

3. In clause (3) of article 280 of the Constitution, after sub-clause, (b), the following sub-clause shall be inserted, namely—

"(bb) the measures needed to augment the Consolidated Fund of a State to supplement the resources of the Panchayats in the State on the basis of the recommendations made by the Finance Commission of the State";

Addition of Eleventh Schedule.

4. After the Tenth Schedule to the Constitution, the following Schedule shall be added, namely—

"ELEVENTH SCHEDULE

(Article 243G)

1. Agriculture, including agricultural extension.
2. Land improvement, implementation of land reforms, land consolidation and soil conservation.
3. Minor irrigation, water management and watershed development.
4. Animal husbandry, dairying and poultry.
5. Fisheries.
6. Social forestry and farm forestry.
7. Minor forest produce
8. Small scale industries, including food processing industries.
9. Khadi, village and cottage industries.
10. Rural housing.
11. Drinking water.
12. Fuel and fodder.
13. Roads, culverts, bridges, ferries, waterways and other means of communication.
14. Rural electrification, including distribution of electricity.
15. Non-conventional energy sources.
16. Poverty alleviation programme.
17. Education, including primary and secondary schools.
18. Technical training and vocational education.
19. Adult and non-formal education.
20. Libraries.
21. Cultural activities.
22. Markets and fairs.

23. Health and sanitation, including hospitals, primary health centres and dispensaries.

24. Family welfare.

25. Women and child development.

26. Social welfare including welfare of the handicapped and mentally retarded.

27. Welfare of the weaker sections, and in particular, of the Scheduled Castes and the Scheduled Tribes.

28. Public distribution system.

29. Maintenance of community assets."

APPENDIX VI

THE CONSTITUTION (SEVENTY-FOURTH AMENDMENT) ACT, 1992

AN ACT

further to amend the Constitution of India

Be it enacted by Parliament in the Forty-third Year of the Republic of India as follows—

Short title and commencement. 1. (1) This act may be called the Constitution (Seventy-fourth Amendment) Act, 1992.

(2) It shall come into force on such date as the Central Government may, by notification in the Official Gazette, appoint.

2. After Part IX of the Constitution, the following Part shall be inserted, namely—

PART IXA

THE MUNICIPALITIES

Definitions. 243P. In this Part, unless the context otherwise requires,—

(a) "Committee" means a Committee constituted under article 243S;

(b) "district" means a district in a State;

(c) "Metropolitan area" means an area having a population of ten lakhs or more comprised in one or more districts and consisting of two or more Municipalities or Panchayats or other contiguous areas, specified by the Governor by public notification to be a Metropolitan area for the purposes of this Part;

(d) "Municipal area" means the territorial areas of a municipality as is notified by the Governor;

(e) "Municipality" means an institution of self-government constituted under article 243Q;

(f) "Panchayat" means a Panchayat constituted under article 243B;

(g) "Population" means the population as ascertained at the last preceding census of which the relevant figures have been published.

Constitution of Municipalities.

243Q.(1) There shall be constituted in every State,—

(a) a Nagar Panchayat (by whatever name called) for a transitional area, that is to say, an area in transition from a rural area to an urban area;

(b) a Municipal Council for a smaller urban area; and

(c) a Municipal Corporation for a larger urban area, in accordance with the provisions of this Part:

Provided that a Municipality under this clause may not be constituted in such urban area or part thereof as the Governor may having regard to the size of the area and the municipal services being provided or proposed to be provided by an industrial establishment in that area and such other factors as he may deem fit, by public notification specify to be an industrial township.

(2) In this article. "a transitional area" a "smaller urban area" or "a larger urban area" means such area as the Governor may, having regard to the population of the area, the density of the population therein, the revenue generated for local administration, the percentage of employment in non-agricultural activities, the economic importance or such other factors as he may deem fit specify by public notification for the purposes of this part.

Composition of Municipalities.

243R. (1) Save as provided in clause (2) all the seats in a Municipality shall be filled by persons chosen by direct election from the territorial constituencies in the Municipal area and for this purpose each Municipal area shall be divided into territorial constituencies to be known as wards.

(2) The Legislature of a State may, by law, provide—

(a) for the representation in a Municipality of—

(i) persons having special knowledge or experience in Municipal administration;

(ii) the members of the House of the People and the members of the Legislative Assembly of the State representing constituencies which comprise wholly or partly the Municipal area;

(iii) the members of the Council of States and the members of the Legislative Council of the State registered as electors within the Municipal area;

(iv) the Chairpersons of the Committees constituted under clause (5) of article 243S:

Provided that the persons referred to in paragraph (i) shall not have the right to vote in the meetings of the Municipality;

(b) the manner of election of the Chairperson of Municipality.

Constitution and composition of Wards Committees, etc.

243S. (1) There shall be constituted Wards Committees, consisting of one or more wards, within the territorial area of a Municipality having a population of three lakhs or more.

(2) The Legislature of a State may, by law, make provision with respect to—

(a) the composition and the territorial area of a Wards Committee;

(b) the member in which the seats in a Wards Committee shall be filled.

(3) A member of a Municipality representing a ward within the territorial area of the Wards Committee shall be a member of that Committee.

(4) Where a Wards Committee consists of—

(a) one ward, the member representing that ward in the Municipality; or

(b) two or more wards, one of the members representing such wards in the Municipality elected by the members of the Wards Committee.

shall be the Chairperson of that Committee.

(5) Nothing in this article shall be deemed to prevent the Legislature of a State from making any provision for the constitution of Committees in addition to the Wards Committees.

Reservation of seats.

243T. (1) Seats shall be reserved for the Scheduled Castes and the Scheduled Tribes in every Municipality and the number of seat so reserved shall bear, as nearly as may be, the same proportion to the total number of seats to be filled by direct election in that Municipality as the population of the Scheduled Castes in the Municipal area or of the Scheduled Tribes in the Municipal area bears to the total population of that area and such seats may be allotted by rotation to different constituencies in a Municipality.

(2) Not less than one-third of the total number of seats reserved under clause (1) shall be reserved for women belonging to the Scheduled Castes or, as the case may be, the Scheduled Tribes.

(3) Not less than one-third (including the number of seats reserved for women belonging to the Scheduled Castes and the Scheduled Tribes) of the total number of seats to be filled by direct election in every Municipality shall be reserved for women and such seats may be allotted by rotation to different constituencies in a Municipality.

(4) The office of Chairpersons in the Municipalities shall be reserved for the Scheduled Castes, the Scheduled Tribes and women in such manner as the Legislature of a State may, by law, provide.

(5) The reservation of seats under clauses (1) and (2) and the reservation of office of Chairpersons (other than the reservation for women under clause (4) shall cease to have effect on the expiration of the period specified in article 334.

(6) Nothing in this Part shall prevent the Legislature of a State from making any provision for reservation of seats in any Municipality or office of Chairpersons in the Municipalities in favour of backward class of citizens.

Duration of Municipalities, etc.

243U. (1) Every Municipality, unless sooner dissolved under any law for the time being in force, shall continue for five years from the date appointed for its first meeting and no longer;

Provided that a Municipality shall be given a reasonable opportunity of being heard before its dissolution.

(2) No amendment of any law for the time being in force shall have the effect of causing dissolution of a Municipality at any level, which is functioning immediately before such amendment, till the expiration of its duration specified in clause (1).

(3) An election to constitute a Municipality shall be completed,—

(a) before the expiry of its duration specified in clause (1);

(b) before the expiration of a period of six months from the date of its dissolution:

Provided that where the reminder of the period for which the dissolved Municipality would have continued is less than six months, it shall not be necessary to hold any election under this clause for constituting the Municipality for such period.

(4) A Municipality constituted upon the dissolution of a Municipality before the expiration of its duration shall continue only for the remainder of the period for which the dissolved Municipality would have continued under clause (1) had it not been so dissolved.

Disqualifications for membership.

243V. (1) A person shall be disqualified for being chosen as, and for being, a member of a Municipality—

(a) if he is so disqualified by or under any law for the time being in force for the purposes of elections to the Legislature of the State concerned:

Provided that no person shall be disqualified on the ground that he is less than twenty-five years of age, if he has attained the age of twenty-one years;

(b) if he is so disqualified by or under any law made by the Legislature of the State.

(2) If any question arises as to whether a member of a Municipality has become subject to any of the disqualifications mentioned in clause (1), the question shall be referred for the decision of such authority and in such manner as the Legislature of a State may, by law, provide.

Powers, authority and responsibilities of Municipalities, etc.

243W. Subject to the provisions of this Constitution, the Legislature of a State may, by law, endow—

(a) the Municipalities with such powers and authority as may be necessary to enable them to function as institutions of self-government and such law may contain provisions for the devolution of powers and responsibilities upon Municipalities, subject to such conditions as may be specified therein, with respect to—

(i) the preparation of plans for economic development and social justice;

(ii) the performance of functions and the implementation of schemes as may be entrusted to them including those in relation to the matters listed in the Twelfth Schedule;

(b) the Committees with such powers and authority as may be necessary to enable them to carry out the responsibilities conferred upon them including those in relation to the matters listed in the Twelfth Schedule.

Powers to impose taxes by and Funds of the Municipalities.

243X. The Legislature of a State may, by law,—

(a) authorise a Municipality to levy, collect and appropriate such taxes, duties, tolls and fees in accordance with such procedure and subject to such limits;

(b) assign to a Municipality such taxes, dutie, tolls and fees levied and collected by the State Government for such purposes and subject to such conditions and limits;

(c) provide for making such grants-in-aid to the Municipalities from the Consolidated Fund of the State; and

(d) provide for constitution of such Funds for crediting all moneys received, respectively, by or on behalf of the Municipalities and also for the withdrawal of such moneys therefrom,

as may be specified in the law.

Finance Commission.

243Y.(1) The Finance Commission constituted under article 243-I shall also review the financial position of the Municipalities and make recommendations to the Governor as to—

(a) the principles which should govern—

(i) the distribution between the State and the Municipalities of the net proceeds of the taxes, duties, tolls and fees leviable by the State, which may be divided between them under this Part and the allocation between the Municipalities at all levels of their respective shares of such proceeds;

(ii) the determination of the taxes, duties, tolls and fees which may be assigned to, or appropriated by, the Municipalities;

(iii) the grants-in-aid to the Municipalities from the Consolidated Fund of the State;

(b) the measures needed to improve the financial position of the Municipalities.

(c) any other matter referred to the Finance Commission by the Governor in the interests of sound finance of the Municipalities.

(2) The Governor shall cause every recommendation made by the Commission under this article together with an explanatory memorandum as to the action taken thereon to be laid before the Legislature of the State.

Audit of accounts of Municipalities.

243Z. The Legislature of a State may, by law, make provisions with respect to the maintenance of accounts by the Municipalities and the audit of such accounts.

Elections to the Municipalities.

243ZA. (1) The superintendence, direction and control of the preparation of electoral rolls for, and the conduct of, all elections to the Municipalities shall be vested in the State Election Commission referred to in article 243K.

(2) Subject to the provisions of this Constitution, the Legislature of a State may, by law, make provision with respect to all matters relating to or in connection with elections to the Municipalities.

Application to Union Territories.

243ZB. The provisions of this Part shall apply to the Union territories and shall, in their application to a Union territory, have effect as if the references to the Governor of a State were references to the Administrator of the Union territory appointed under article 239 and references to the Legislature or the Legislative Assembly of a State were references in relation to a Union territory having a Legislative Assembly, to that Legislative Assembly:

Provided that the President may by public notification, direct that the provisions of this Part shall apply to any Union territory or part thereof subject to such exceptions and modifications as he may specify in the notification.

Part not to apply to certain areas. 243ZC. (1) Nothing in this Part shall apply to the Scheduled Areas referred to in clause (1), and the tribal areas referred to in clause (2), of article 244.

(2) Nothing in this Part shall be construed to affect the functions ad powers of the Darjeeling Gorkha Hill Council constituted under any law for the time being in force for the hill areas of the district of Darjeeling in the State of West Bengal.

(3) Notwithstanding anything in this Constitution, Parliament may, by law, extend the provisions of this Part to the Scheduled Areas and the tribal areas referred to in clause (1) subject to such exceptions and modifications as may be specified in such law, and no such law shall be deemed to be an amendment of this Constitution for the purposes of article 368.

Committee for district planning. 243ZD. (1) There shall be constituted in every State at the district level a District Planning Committee to consolidate the plans prepared by the Panchayats and the Municipalities in the district and to prepare a draft development plan for the district as a whole.

(2) The Legislature of a State may, by law, make provision with respect to—

(a) the composition of the District Planning Committees;

(b) the manner in which the seats in such Committees shall be filled:

Provided that not less than four-fifths of the total number of members of such Committee shall be elected by, and from amongst, the elected members of the Panchayat at the district level and of the Municipalities in the district in proportion to the ratio between the population of the rural areas and of the urban areas in the district;

(c) the functions relating to district planning which may be assigned to such Committees;

(d) the manner in which the Chairpersons of such Committees shall be chosen.

(3) Every District Planning Committee shall, in preparing the draft development plan,—

(a) have regard to—

(i) matters of common interest between the Panchayats and the Municipalities including spatial planning, sharing of water and other physical and natural resources, the integrated development of infrastructure and environmental conservation;

(ii) the extent and type of available resources whether financial or otherwise;

(b) consult such institutions and organisations as the Governor may, by order, specify.

(4) The Chairperson of every District Planning Committee shall forward the development plan, as recommended by such Committee, to the Government of the State.

Committee for Metropolitan planning.

243ZE. (1) There shall be constituted in every Metropolitan area a Metropolitan Planning Committee to prepare a draft development plan for the Metropolitan area as a whole.

(2) The Legislature of a State may, by law, make provision with respect to—

(a) the composition of the Metropolitan Planning Committees;

(b) the manner in which the seats in such Committees shall be filled:

Provided that not less than two-thirds of the members of such Committee shall be elected by, and from amongst, the elected members of the Municipalities and Chairpersons of the Panchayats in the Metropolitan area in proportion to the ratio between the population of the Municipalities and of the Panchayats in that area;

(c) the representation in such Committees of the Government of India and the Government of the State and of such organisations and institutions as may be deemed necessary for carrying out the functions assigned to such Committees;

(d) the functions relating to planning and coordination for the Metropolitan area which may be assigned to such Committees;

(e) the manner in which the Chairpersons of such Committees shall be chosen.

(3) Every Metropolitan Planning Committee shall, in preparing the draft development plan,—

(a) have regard to—

(i) the plans prepared by the Municipalities and the Panchayats in the Metropolitan area;

(b) matters of common interest between the Municipalities and the Panchayats including co-ordinated spatial planning of the area, sharing of water and other physical and natural resources, the integrated development of infrastructure and environmental conservation;

(iii) the overall objectives and priorities set by the Government of India and the Government of the State;

(iv) the extent and nature of investments likely to be made in the Metropolitan area by agencies of the Government of India and of the Government of the State and other available resources whether financial or otherwise;

(b) consult such institutions and organisations as the Governor may, by order, specify.

(4) The Chairperson of every Metropolitan Planning Committee shall forward the development plan, as recommended by such Committee, to the Government of the States.

Continuance of existing laws and Municipalities.

243ZF. Notwithstanding anything in this Part, any provisions of any law relating to Municipalities in force in a State immediately before the commencement of the Constitution Seventy-fourth Amendment) Act, 1992, which is inconsistent with the provisions of this Part, shall continue to be in force until amended or repealed by a competent Legislature, or other competent authority or until the expiration of one year from such commencement, whichever is earlier.

Provided that all the Municipalities existing immediately before such commencement shall continue till the expiration of their duration, unless sooner dissolved by a resolution passed to that effect by the Legislative Assembly of that State or, in the case of a State having a Legislative Council, by each House of the Legislature of that State.

Ban on interference by courts in electoral matters.

243ZG. Notwithstanding anything in this Constitution—

(a) the validity of any law relating to the delimitation of constituencies or the allotment of seats to such constituencies, made or purporting to be made under article 243ZA shall not be called in question in any court;

(b) no election to any Municipality shall be called in question except by an election petition presented to such authority and in such manner as is provided for by or under any law made by the Legislature of a State.

Amendment of article 280.

3. In clause (3) of article 280 of the Constitution, sub-clause (c) shall be lettered as sub-clause (d) and before sub-clause (d) as so relettered, the following sub-clause shall be inserted, namely—

"(c) the measures needed to augment the Consolidated Fund of a State to supplement the resources of the Municipalities in the State on the basis of the recommendations made by the Finance Commission of the State;"

Agenda of Twelfth Schedule.

4. After the Eleventh Schedule to the Constitution, the following Schedule shall be added, namely—

"TWELFTH SCHEDULE

(Article 243W)

1. Urban Planning including town planning.
2. Regulation of Land-use and construction of buildings.
3. Planning for economic and social development.
4. Roads and bridges.
5. Water supply for domestic, industrial and commercial purposes.

6. Public health, sanitation conservancy and solid waste management.
7. Fire services
8. Urban forestry, protection of the environment and promotion of ecological aspects.
9. Safeguarding the interests of weaker sections of society, including the handicapped and mentally retarded.
10. Slum improvement and upgradation.
11. Urban poverty alleviation.
12. Provision of urban amenities and facilities such as parks, gardens, playgrounds.
13. Promotion of cultural, educational and aesthetic aspects.
14. Burials and burial grounds; cremations, cremation grounds and electric crematoriums.
15. Cattle pounds; prevention of cruelty to animals.
16. Vital statistics including registration of births and deaths.
17. Public amenities including street lighting, parking lots, bus stops and public conveniences.
18. Regulation of slaughter houses and tanneries."